THE DEVIL'S FOOD™
A DESSERT COOKBOOK

written by
HOLLY BERKOWITZ CLEGG

photography by
DAVID PRITCHARD

Holly Berkowitz Clegg is a graduate of Sophie Newcomb College. She attended the Cordon Bleu Cooking School in London. In Paris, she attended classes at the Cordon Bleu Cooking School and La Varenne.

Also by Holly Clegg

A Trim & Terrific Louisiana Kitchen
Trim & Terrific American Favorites
Trim & Terrific One Dish Favorites

Nutrient Analysis by
Dr. Carolyn Gibbons
Louisiana State University

Photography by
David Pritchard
Cookbook designed and coordinated
by Elizabeth Neely

On the Cover:
Raspberry Sauce, p. 147
Delicious Cheesecake, p. 124

ISBN 1-58209-047-5

Special Edition for Books Are Fun Ltd

Library of Congress Catalog Card
Number 88-62596

Printed in China

JUST A NOTE

SPLURGE!! At the end of a meal, there is always room for dessert. Don't we always save the best for last? Back by popular demand, I have reprinted my cookbook, ***The Devil's Food: A Dessert Cookbook***. Whenever you want to indulge yourself, this book offers sensational recipes that will satisfy any sweet tooth in any time limit. As in my other cookbooks, most ingredients can be found in any pantry to create the treat of your choice. For those who feel time is a factor, the ***Quick and Easy*** section contains recipes that take little time and effort, yet they are terrific. My ***Spectacular Endings*** section allows the adventurous baker to use practical recipes to create decadent desires. Other sections that includes all time favorites are the ***Cookies*** and ***Bar Cookies, Cakes, Pies, and Candies***. For those who want an impressive and delicious health conscious dessert, the *Trim & Terrific* section will be the one for you. I am excited to share some of my new *Trim & Terrific* recipes that are absolutely fabulous. By keeping this dessert cookbook in your kitchen, you too, can have <u>new</u> and wonderful ideas to offer your family and friends when you decide to **SPLURGE!**

Have fun cooking,

Holly Berkowitz Clegg

TABLE OF CONTENTS

PHOTOGRAPHS

Quick
and Easy

Lemon Squares

1	(18½-ounce) package lemon cake mix with pudding
3	eggs
1	cup chopped pecans
½	cup butter, melted
1	(8-ounce) package cream cheese, softened
1	(16-ounce) box powdered sugar
1	teaspoon vanilla

In a large mixing bowl, combine cake mix, 1 egg, pecans, and melted butter. Beat by hand until well blended. Pat batter into the bottom of a lightly greased 13×9×2-inch baking pan. In mixing bowl, beat cream cheese, powdered sugar, and 2 eggs together until mixture is smooth and creamy. Add vanilla. Pour over batter in pan. Bake at 350 degrees for 45 minutes or until top is golden brown. Cool and cut into squares.

Loaded Bars

1	(20-ounce) roll refrigerator chocolate chip cookie dough
1	(14-ounce) package caramels
¼	cup milk
1	(6-ounce) package semi-sweet chocolate chips
1	cup chopped pecans

Cut cookie dough ¼-inch thick and press into a 13×9×2-inch baking pan. Bake at 375 degrees for 10 minutes or until light brown. While baking, combine caramels and milk in top of double boiler, cooking until caramels are melted. (Can microwave if desired, but watch carefully). When cookie dough is done, cool slightly. Sprinkle with chocolate chips and drizzle warm caramel mixture on top of chocolate chips. Top with pecans and refrigerate. Cut into squares.

NOTE: Quick and so good.

Chocolate Praline Bars

¾ cup butter
1½ cups light brown sugar
12 whole graham crackers
1½ cups mini semi-sweet chocolate
     chips

½ cup peanut butter chips
1   cup chopped pecans

Combine butter and brown sugar in saucepan until comes to a boil. Remove from heat. Line a 15 × 10 × 2-inch jelly roll pan with graham crackers. Sprinkle with chocolate and peanut butter chips and pecans. Pour cooked butter mixture evenly on top of chips and pecans. Bake at 375 degrees for 8 to 10 minutes or until bars are bubbly.

NOTE: These are simple to make and the ingredients are usually in your pantry. Can substitute chips of your choice.

Fudgy Fluff Bars

1   (18½-ounce) box fudge cake
     mix
½ cup butter, softened
2   tablespoons water
1   (7.2-ounce) package fluffy white
     frosting mix

½ cup boiling water
½ cup chopped pecans
½ cup semi-sweet chocolate chips

In large bowl, combine the cake mix, butter, and water. Stir by hand until well mixed. (Batter will be stiff). Press into ungreased 13 × 9 × 2-inch baking pan. Prepare frosting with boiling water as directed on package. Spread frosting on unbaked fudge base. Sprinkle pecans and chocolate chips over frosting. Bake at 350 degrees for 20 to 25 minutes until toothpick inserted near edge of bars comes out clean. Cool.

Quick Chocolate Chip Bars

2 **(20-ounce) packages chocolate chip slice and bake cookie dough**	2 **cups sugar**
3 **eggs, beaten**	2 **(8-ounce) packages cream cheese**

Press one roll of cookie dough into the bottom of a greased and floured 13×9×2-inch baking pan. Set aside. Beat eggs with sugar until creamy. Stir in cream cheese and beat until well blended. Spread over cookie dough. Slice the second package of cookie dough into thin slices and cover cream cheese layer with them. Bake at 350 degrees for 40 to 45 minutes.

Easy German Chocolate Cake

1 **(4-ounce) package German sweet chocolate**	4 **eggs**
1 **(18½-ounce) box yellow cake mix**	¼ **cup oil**
	1¼ **cups buttermilk**
1 **(4-servings) package instant vanilla pudding**	1 **(6-ounce) package semi-sweet chocolate chips**

In top of double boiler or in microwave, melt chocolate. Cool. In mixing bowl, combine all ingredients, mixing well. Pour batter into a greased and floured 13×9×2-inch baking pan. Bake at 325 degrees for 30 minutes. Cool. Cover with Topping (see recipe below).

Topping:

1 **cup evaporated milk**	1 **teaspoon vanilla**
1 **cup sugar**	1 **cup chopped pecans**
3 **egg yolks, slightly beaten**	1 **cup flaked coconut**
½ **cup butter**	

In heavy saucepan, combine milk, sugar, egg yolks, and butter. Cook over medium heat, stirring until the mixture thickens (about 12 minutes). Remove from heat, add vanilla. Add pecans and coconut. Let topping cool. Spread on top of cake.

NOTE: After this recipe, you will never go to the trouble of a German Chocolate Cake made from scratch.

Coconut Pecan Cake

1	cup chopped pecans	¾	cup oil
1½	cups flaked coconut	½	cup butter, melted
3	tablespoons light brown sugar	4	eggs
1	(18½-ounce) butter flavored cake mix	1	cup buttermilk

In small bowl, combine pecans, coconut, and brown sugar. Set aside. In large mixing bowl, combine remaining ingredients, beating until combined. Spread half of batter into a greased and floured 13×9×2-inch baking pan. Pour ¾cup of coconut/pecan mixture over batter. Top with remaining batter. Bake at 325 degrees for 40 to 45 minutes. Cool and ice with Cream Cheese Frosting (see recipe below). Then sprinkle remaining coconut/pecan mixture over iced cake.

Cream Cheese Frosting:

1	(8-ounce) package cream cheese	1	(16-ounce) box powdered sugar
¼	cup butter	1	teaspoon vanilla

In mixing bowl, beat the cream cheese and butter together. Blend in powdered sugar, mixing well. Add vanilla. Ice cake.

NOTE: This cake tastes like a very involved cake because it's so good.

Quick Cake

4	eggs	2	cups chopped pecans
1	(16-ounce) box light brown sugar	1	(6-ounce) package semi-sweet chocolate chips
2	cups biscuit baking mix		

In large bowl, combine all ingredients, mixing well. Pour into a greased and floured 13×9×2-inch baking pan. Bake at 300 degrees for 45 minutes. Cool in pan for 15 minutes before cutting.

Amaretto Cake

1	(18½-ounce) box yellow cake mix	¼	cup vodka
1	(4-serving) box instant pistachio pudding	¼	cup Amaretto
		⅔	cup orange juice
¾	cup oil	4	eggs

In large bowl, blend all ingredients together except eggs. Add eggs, one at a time, beating well after each addition. Pour into a greased and floured 10-inch bundt pan. Bake at 350 degrees for 45 to 55 minutes. Prepare the Glaze (see recipe below) during the last 5 minutes of baking. Pour over cake and let it stand for 30 minutes in pan. Invert onto serving plate. Sprinkle with powdered sugar.

Glaze:

1	cup sugar	¼	cup orange juice
½	cup butter, melted	¼	cup Amaretto

Mix well and spread over cake after removing from oven.

Sherry Pound Cake

1	(18½-ounce) box yellow cake mix	1	cup oil
		¾	cup cream sherry
1	(4-serving) box instant vanilla pudding	4	eggs
		½	cup chopped pecans

Combine cake mix and pudding in a large mixing bowl. Add oil and sherry. Add eggs, one at a time, beating well after each addition. Beat for 5 minutes. Add pecans. Pour into greased and floured 10-inch bundt pan and bake at 350 degrees for 45 minutes. Cover with Glaze (see recipe below).

Glaze:

1	cup powdered sugar	¼	cup cream sherry

Combine sugar and sherry. Drizzle one-third of glaze over hot cake in pan. Cool 15 minutes and turn out on serving plate. Drizzle rest of glaze on top of cake and let run down sides.

Quick Blueberry Pound Cake

1	(18½-ounce) box golden yellow cake mix	3	eggs
1	(8-ounce) package cream cheese, softened	1	teaspoon vanilla
½	cup oil	2	cups blueberries
		1	cup chopped pecans

In large mixing bowl, mix all ingredients together except blueberries and pecans. Fold in blueberries and pecans. Pour batter into a greased and floured 10-inch bundt pan. Bake at 350 degrees for 50 to 60 minutes. Cool in pan for 20 minutes, invert, and sprinkle with powdered sugar.

Mandarin Orange Cake

1	(18½-ounce) box yellow cake mix	1	cup oil
4	eggs	1	(11-ounce) can mandarin oranges with juice

Place all ingredients in bowl and mix for 2 minutes. Pour batter into two greased and floured 9-inch round baking pans. Bake at 350 degrees for 15 to 20 minutes or until done. Cool and then frost with Frosting (see recipe below).

Frosting:

1	(20-ounce) can crushed pineapple with juice	½	teaspoon vanilla
1	(4-serving) package instant French vanilla pudding	1	(8-ounce) container whipped topping

Whip pineapple and pudding together with spoon. Add vanilla. Fold in whipped topping. Spread frosting between layers, sides, and on top of cake.

NOTE: An easy and refreshing cake. Good on a hot day.

Strawberry Cake

1	cup oil	1	(4-serving) strawberry gelatin
1	cup crushed fresh strawberries or one-half (10-ounce) package frozen strawberries and juice, thawed	4	eggs
		½	teaspoon vanilla
		¼	teaspoon butter flavoring
		1	cup flaked coconut
½	cup milk	1	cup chopped pecans
1	(18½-ounce) box white cake mix		

In large bowl, combine oil, strawberries, and milk. Mix cake mix with gelatin and add to strawberry mixture. Beat well. Add eggs, mixing well. Add flavorings, coconut, and pecans. Pour into three greased and floured 9-inch round cake pans. Bake at 350 degrees for 20 to 25 minutes or until cake springs up when touched. Remove from pan. After cake is cooled, spread with Strawberry Frosting (see recipe below).

Strawberry Frosting:

Dash salt		1	teaspoon vanilla
½	cup butter	½	teaspoon butter flavoring
1½	(16-ounce) boxes powdered sugar	½	cup flaked coconut
		½	cup chopped pecans
½	cup crushed strawberries or one-half (10-ounce) package frozen strawberries and juice, thawed		

In mixing bowl, combine all ingredients together except coconut and pecans. Stir in coconut and pecans. Mix well and frost cooled cake.

Easy Angel Food Strawberry Cake

1	(12-ounce) angel food cake	½	cup powdered sugar
1	quart fresh strawberries,	1	teaspoon vanilla
	stemmed	2	(8-ounce) containers whipped
3	tablespoons sugar		topping
1	(8-ounce) package cream cheese,	¾	cup Amaretto
	softened	⅓	cup sliced almonds, toasted

Slice angel food cake horizontally into three layers. Slice strawberries and put in bowl. Sprinkle with sugar and gently toss to mix well. Refrigerate strawberries for 30 minutes. In large mixing bowl, combine cream cheese and powdered sugar, blending well. Add vanilla. Gradually add one (8-ounce) container whipped topping, beating until smooth. Fold in other 8-ounce container, mixing until combined. Sprinkle bottom layer with ¼ cup Amaretto, then with whipped cream cheese mixture, and then with fresh sliced strawberries. Repeat with remaining layers. Frost sides and top of cake with remaining cream cheese mixture. Garnish with sliced almonds. Refrigerate. Yield: 8 to 12 servings.

NOTE: This colorfully delicious dessert freezes well.

Sour Cream Coconut Cake

1	(18½-ounce) box butter cake mix	⅓	cup oil
1	(4-serving) box instant vanilla pudding	1	(18-ounce) can coconut in heavy syrup
4	eggs	1	cup sour cream
1	cup water	1	(8-ounce) container whipped topping

Mix together cake mix, vanilla pudding, eggs, water, and oil. Pour into three greased and floured 9-inch round pans. Bake at 350 degrees for 25 minutes. Cool and invert on cooling racks. Mix coconut in heavy syrup and sour cream together in small bowl. Reserve 1 cup and set aside. Spread coconut and sour cream mixture between cake layers. Mix the 1 cup reserved coconut and sour cream mixture with the whipped topping and frost the cake. Refrigerate.

NOTE: The longer it sits, the better it gets, if it lasts that long.

Crunchy Quick Peach Cobber

3	cups thinly sliced peaches, peeled and cored	1	cup sugar
1	tablespoon lemon juice	1	egg
1	cup self-rising flour	½	cup butter, melted

Place sliced peaches in a lightly buttered dish. Sprinkle with lemon juice. In bowl, combine flour, sugar, and egg, mixing well. Crumble over peaches. Pour melted butter on top of crust. Bake at 375 degrees for 30 to 35 minutes.

NOTE: For those who do not like to make a crust, this cobbler is for you. It is so good to be so easy. Any fruit can be substituted.

Pineapple Trifle

2   (8-ounce) packages cream cheese
1   cup sugar
1   cup evaporated milk
1   (16-ounce) angel food cake, cubed
1   (20-ounce) can crushed pineapple, including juice

2   tablespoons cornstarch
2   cups coarsely chopped pecans
1   (12-ounce) container whipped topping

In mixing bowl, beat cream cheese, sugar, and evaporated milk. Mix with cubed angel food cake. In small saucepan, combine pineapple and cornstarch. Cook over low heat until thick, stirring constantly. Set aside. In a trifle dish, layer half of angel food cake mixture, pineapple mixture, pecans, and whipped topping. Repeat again, ending with whipped topping. Refrigerate.

NOTE: This dessert makes a statement and it takes so little time to make.

Chocolate Eclair Dessert

1   (16-ounce) box graham crackers
2   (4-serving) packages French vanilla instant pudding

3   cups milk
1   (8-ounce) container whipped topping

Layer bottom of a buttered 13×9×2-inch baking pan with one-third of graham crackers. In bowl, beat pudding mix with milk. Fold in whipped topping. Spread half of pudding mixture over graham crackers. Repeat layers, ending with graham crackers on top. Spread with Chocolate Topping (see recipe below).

Chocolate Topping:

2   (1-ounce) squares unsweetened chocolate
3   tablespoons butter

1½ cups powdered sugar
1   teaspoon vanilla
2   tablespoons light corn syrup

Melt chocolate and butter in top of double boiler or microwave. Mix with remaining ingredients, stirring until smooth. Spread on top. Refrigerate for 24 hours if can before serving.

NOTE: This is such an easy and delicious copy of an eclair, you won't want the real thing.

Ice Cream Pie

1¼ cups graham cracker crumbs
¼ cup sugar
¼ cup butter, melted
1 cup coffee ice cream or cookies
  'n cream ice cream, softened
1 cup milk

1 (4-serving) package vanilla
  instant pudding
1 (8-ounce) container whipped
  topping
Pecans for garnish

Combine graham cracker crumbs, sugar, and melted butter. Pat crumb mixture into a 9-inch pie plate. Bake at 325 degrees 10 minutes or until browned. Cool. In a bowl blend lightly together ice cream and milk. Add instant pudding and beat until just mixed. Pour at once into prepared crust. Refrigerate about 2 hours. Top with whipped topping and sprinkle with pecans.

NOTE: Use your favorite ice cream to create the pie of your choice. Easy.

Easy Chocolate Bar Pie

Crust:
2 cups chocolate wafer crumbs   ¼ cup butter, melted

Combine ingredients and press into the bottom of a 9-inch pie plate. Fill crust with Chocolate Filling (see recipe below).

4 (1.65-ounce) milk chocolate
  candy bars
2 (1.45-ounce) dark chocolate
  candy bars (mildly sweet)

1 (12-ounce) container whipped
  topping
1 cup chopped pecans, toasted

Melt chocolate candy bars in top of double boiler or in microwave. Fold into half container whipped topping, combining until thoroughly mixed. Fold in ¾ cup toasted pecans. Spread chocolate filling on top of crust. Carefully spread remaining whipped topping over chocolate filling in pie. Garnish with remaining ¼ cup chopped pecans and shaved chocolate. Refrigerate.

NOTE: All ages are ready to eat a piece of this pie.

Chocolate Cake with Peanut Butter Filling

1 (18½-ounce) package devil's food cake mix	¼ cup milk
	1 egg
½ cup butter, melted	¾ cup dry roasted peanuts

In large mixing bowl, combine all ingredients except peanuts and beat until well blended. Add peanuts. Spread batter into a greased and floured 13×9×2-inch baking pan. Bake at 350 degrees for 20 minutes. DO NOT OVERBAKE. Cool. Top with Peanut Butter Filling (see recipe below).

Peanut Butter Filling:

¾ cup peanut butter	1 (6-serving) package instant vanilla pudding and pie filling
1½ cups powdered sugar	
1 (8-ounce) package cream cheese, softened	1 (1.65-ounce) milk chocolate candy bar, grated
2½ cups milk	½ cup dry roasted peanuts
1 (8-ounce) container whipped topping	

In small bowl, combine peanut butter and powdered sugar at low speed until crumbly; set aside. In large bowl, beat cream cheese until smooth. Gradually add milk, whipped topping, and pudding; beat 2 minutes at low speed until well blended.

Pour half of cream cheese mixture over cooled cake. Sprinkle with half of crumbly peanut butter mixture. Repeat with remaining cream cheese and peanut butter mixtures. Sprinkle with grated chocolate and peanuts. Refrigerate.

NOTE: This is a fudgy cake with a fluffy peanut butter filling.

23

Mocha Fudge Mousse Pie

Brownie Crust:

¼ cup water	¼ cup oil
1 teaspoon instant coffee	1 egg
1 (12.9-ounce) box fudge brownie mix	½ cup coarsely chopped pecans

In a small glass measuring cup, stir together the water and coffee until the powder dissolves. In a large bowl, combine the brownie mix, oil, egg, and coffee mixture with a large spoon and stir for 1 minute, until combined. Stir in the pecans. Scrape the batter into a lightly buttered 9-inch pie plate and bake at 350 degrees for 28 to 32 minutes, until a cake tester or toothpick inserted into the center comes out clean. Do not overbake. Cool the brownie crust completely in the pan on a wire rack. Spread Mousse (see recipe below) over crust.

Mousse:

1 cup milk	1 (3.5-ounce) box chocolate fudge mousse mix
1 tablespoon coffee liqueur	
1 teaspoon instant coffee	

In a medium bowl, stir together the milk, liqueur, and coffee until the coffee is almost dissolved and add the mousse mix. Beat just until blended. Beat at high speed for 3 minutes, until the mixture thickens. Place mousse in freezer until the mousse is firm enough to mound. Spread the mousse over the brownie curst, mounding it slightly in the center. Return the pie to the freezer for 15 minutes, until firm enough to slice. Top with Topping (see recipe below). Refrigerate.

Topping:

1 (8-ounce) container whipped topping	1 tablespoon coffee liqueur

Combine whipped topping and liqueur together. Cover top of pie with mixture.

NOTE: This is a superb chocolate dessert!

Blueberry Crumble

1   (13-ounce) box wild blueberry
    muffin mix
¼   cup sugar
½   teaspoon cinnamon
¼   cup butter, melted
⅔   cup chopped pecans

2   (16-ounce) cans blueberry pie
    filling
¼   cup sugar
1   teaspoon cinnamon
1   teaspoon almond extract

In a bowl, combine blueberry muffin mix, ¼ cup sugar, and ½ teaspoon cinnamon. Pour melted butter over top. Add pecans, stir, and set aside. In another bowl, combine blueberry pie filling, ¼ cup sugar, 1 teaspoon cinnamon, and almond extract. Pour pie filling mixture into a lightly greased 8 × 8 × 2-inch square baking pan. Sprinkle muffin crumble mixture on top. Bake at 350 degrees for 35 minutes or until top is golden. If desired, serve with whipped topping or ice cream.

NOTE: This is out of this world!

Cookies and
Bar Cookies

Triple Chocolate Clusters

6 (1-ounce) squares semi-sweet chocolate	¼ teaspoon salt
2 (1-ounce) squares unsweetened chocolate	2 eggs
½ cup unsalted butter, cut into ½-inch cubes	2 teaspoons vanilla
	¾ cup sugar
½ cup flour	½ cup coarsely chopped walnuts
1 teaspoon baking powder	½ cup coarsely chopped pecans
	½ cup semi-sweet chocolate chips

In the microwave or in top of a double boiler, melt the semi-sweet and unsweetened chocolates with the butter, stirring constantly until smooth. Remove the pan from the heat. In a small bowl, stir together the flour, baking powder, and salt. In a large bowl, beat the eggs and vanilla until frothy. Gradually add the sugar and continue beating for 4 to 6 minutes, until the mixture forms a thick ribbon when the beaters are lifted. Beat in the warm chocolate mixture. Reduce the speed to low and blend in the flour mixture. Stir in the walnuts, pecans, and chocolate chips. Drop the batter by rounded teaspoons onto greased baking sheets, leaving 2 inches between cookies. Bake at 325 degrees for 10 to 12 minutes, until a cookie feels firm when lightly touched and the tops of the cookies are slightly cracked. The centers of the cookies will be soft and fudgy. Cool the cookies on the baking sheet for 2 to 4 minutes. Transfer the cookies to the rack to cool completely. Yield: approximately 3 dozen.

NOTE: A chocolate lover's cookie — they are light.

Chocolate Drop Cookies

1   (12-ounce) package semi-sweet   ½   cup butter
    chocolate chips   1   cup flour
4   tablespoons sugar   1   cup chopped pecans
1   (14-ounce) can sweetened   1   teaspoon vanilla
    condensed milk

Melt chocolate chips and sugar in top of double boiler or microwave until melted. Add condensed milk and butter. Stir until butter is completely melted. Remove from heat and pour over the flour in a bowl. Mix well and add the pecans and vanilla. Blend well by hand. Put in refrigerator for about an hour before baking (or overnight). The batter will be stiff. Drop by teaspoonfuls onto ungreased cookie sheet and bake at 350 degrees for 8 to 10 minutes or until top of cookie looks like it is "set." As soon as you take them from the oven, remove from cookie sheet and place on wire rack to cool. Yield: 4 to 5 dozen.

NOTE: A super chocolate cookie.

Peanut Butter Cookies

1   egg   1   cup crunchy peanut butter
1   cup sugar   1   teaspoon vanilla

In bowl, mix ingredients well. Roll dough into a ball and place on greased cookie sheets. With the back of a floured fork, press down the ball. Bake at 375 degrees for 10 to 12 minutes. Watch carefully for burning. Remove immediately to rack to cool. Yield: approximately 2 dozen cookies.

NOTE: There is no flour in these cookies. Quick, easy and great.

Crunchy Potato Chip Cookies

2 cups butter	3¼ cups flour
1 cup sugar	1½ cups crushed potato chips
1 teaspoon vanilla	Powdered sugar

In large mixing bowl, beat butter until softened. Add 1 cup sugar and vanilla, beating until fluffy. With mixer on low speed, gradually add flour and crushed potato chips, beating until well mixed. Drop by rounded teaspoons about 2 inches apart onto ungreased cookie sheets. Flatten the dough with a fork that has been dipped in powdered sugar. Bake at 325 degrees for 15 to 20 minutes or until golden. Remove cookies **immediately** from cookie sheets onto waxed paper to cool. Yield: Approximately 5 to 6 dozen cookies.

NOTE: Bet you cannot eat just one of these buttery cookies.

Sugar Cookies

1 cup butter, softened	1 egg
1½ cups powdered sugar	2½ cups flour
1 teaspoon vanilla	1½ teaspoons baking powder
1 teaspoon almond extract, optional	

In large mixing bowl, mix butter and powdered sugar until light and fluffy. Add extracts and egg, beating well. Combine flour and baking powder; add to sugar mixture. Chill dough in refrigerator 3 hours. Roll out on sugared board and cut with floured cutters. Bake at 350 degrees for 8 minutes. Yield: approximately 5 dozen.

NOTE: Use your favorite cookie cutter to make whatever shapes you want.

Orange Pecan Cookies

½ cup shortening	1 tablespoon grated orange rind
⅓ cup sugar	1 tablespoon grated lemon rind
1 egg yolk	1 cup flour
½ teaspoon vanilla	2 eggs whites, unbeaten
⅛ teaspoon salt	1 cup chopped pecans

In mixing bowl, cream shortening, sugar, egg yolk, vanilla, salt, grated orange, and lemon rind. Work in flour. Shape dough in balls the size of walnuts. Roll in unbeaten egg whites and chopped pecans. Place on a greased baking sheet and flatten with a spatula. Bake at 350 degrees for 12 minutes. Yield: 2 to 2½ dozen.

NOTE: These cookies have a wonderful flavor and melt in your mouth.

Macadamia Nut Cookies

½ cup unsalted butter, softened	1 tablespoon vanilla
1 (8-ounce) package cream cheese, softened	1½ cups flour
	2 teaspoons baking powder
¾ cup light brown sugar	1½ cups coarsely chopped
1 teaspoon grated orange rind	macadamia nuts

In a large mixing bowl, beat the butter and cream cheese until light and fluffy. Beat in the brown sugar and then the orange rind and vanilla. Sift the flour and baking powder together and stir into the butter mixture with a wooden spoon. Stir in the macadamia nuts. Refrigerate the dough at least 1 hour or overnight. Drop by heaping teaspoons 2 inches apart onto greased cookie sheets and flatten slightly with the back of a fork which has been dipped in flour. Bake at 400 degrees for 8 to 10 minutes, or until lightly browned. Remove to wire racks to cool completely. Yield: 3 to 4 dozen.

Oatmeal Cookies

½ cup light brown sugar	1 teaspoon baking powder
1 cup sugar	1 teaspoon cinnamon
1 cup butter	½ teaspoon salt
2 eggs	2 cups old fashioned oatmeal
1 teaspoon vanilla	1 cup chopped walnuts
1 teaspoon grated lemon rind	1 cup raisins
2 cups flour	1 teaspoon baking powder
1 teaspoon baking soda	

In mixing bowl, cream sugars and butter until light and fluffy. Add eggs, vanilla, and lemon rind. Combine flour, baking soda, baking powder, cinnamon, and salt together. Add to creamed mixture, mixing well. Stir in oatmeal, walnuts, and raisins. Refrigerate dough for four hours or overnight. Drop by rounded spoonfuls onto ungreased cookie sheet. Bake at 350 degrees for about 10 to 15 minutes. Yield: 3 dozen large cookies or 6 dozen small cookies.

NOTE: This is a cake-like cookie.

Cowboy Cookies

1 cup shortening	1 teaspoon baking powder
½ cup butter	¾ teaspoon salt
1½ cups sugar	3 cups old fashioned oatmeal
1½ cups light brown sugar	2 teaspoons vanilla
3 eggs	1 cup chopped pecans
3 cups flour	1 (12-ounce) package semi-sweet
1½ teaspoons baking soda	chocolate chips

In large mixing bowl, cream shortening, butter, sugar, and brown sugar until light and fluffy. Add eggs, mixing well. Sift together flour, baking soda, baking powder, and salt. Gradually add flour mixture. Stir in pecans and chocolate chips, mixing well. Bake at 350 degrees for 10 to 12 minutes. Do not overbake. Yield: 8 dozen.

NOTE: Freezes well if they will last that long.

Chocolate Chip Cookies

1   cup butter
1   cup sugar
1   cup light brown sugar
2   eggs
1   teaspoon vanilla
2   cups flour
½   teaspoon salt
1   teaspoon baking powder

1   teaspoon baking soda
2½ cups old fashioned oatmeal
1   (12-ounce) package semi-sweet
    chocolate chips
1   (4-ounce) bar German-sweet
    chocolate, grated
1½ cups chopped pecans

In large mixing bowl, cream butter, sugar, and brown sugar together until light and fluffy. Add eggs and vanilla. Combine flour, salt, baking powder, and baking soda. Place oatmeal in food processor and turn it into a powder. Add to flour mixture. Mix flour/oatmeal mixture into creamed mixture. Blend well. Stir in chocolate chips, grated chocolate, and pecans. Bake on ungreased cookie sheets at 375 degrees for 10 to 12 minutes. Yield: Approximately 5 dozen cookies.

NOTE: This chocolate chip cookie is loaded with extras!

Chocolate Chunk Cookies

2   cups flour
1   teaspoon baking soda
½   teaspoon salt
½   cup butter
½   cup shortening
½   cup sugar

¾   cup light brown sugar
1   teaspoon vanilla
1   egg
2   cups semi-sweet chocolate
    chunks
1   cup chopped pecans

In small bowl, combine flour, baking soda, and salt. Set aside. In mixing bowl, combine butter, shortening, sugar, and brown sugar, beating until light and fluffy. Add vanilla and egg, beating well. Gradually add flour mixture, mixing well. Stir in chocolate chunks and pecans. Drop by rounded spoonfuls onto ungreased cookie sheet. Bake at 375 degrees for 8 to 10 minutes. Cool on cookie sheet a few minutes and remove to wire racks to cool completely. Yield: 3 to 4 dozen cookies.

NOTE: This is the ultimate chocolate chunk cookie. Can substitute chocolate chips if desire.

Sand Tarts

1 cup butter, softened	2 cups flour
½ cup powdered sugar (heaping)	½ teaspoon salt
1 teaspoon almond extract	1 cup chopped pecans
1 teaspoon vanilla	Powdered sugar

In mixing bowl, cream butter and sugar until light and fluffy. Add flavorings. Add flour and salt, mixing well. Add pecans. Refrigerate dough for 1 hour. Shape dough into large half moons or crescents. Place on ungreased cookie sheets and bake at 350 degrees for 18 to 22 minutes, or until tops are light brown. When lukewarm, dip into powdered sugar and cool. When cool, dip again into powdered sugar. Cookies freeze very well. Yield: 30 very large sand tarts.

NOTE: This recipe is my Aunt Sonya's and she is known for her sand tarts.

Macaroon Kiss Cookies

⅓ cup butter	1¼ cups flour
1 (3-ounce) package cream cheese	2 teaspoons baking powder
¾ cup sugar	¼ teaspoon salt
1 egg yolk	4 cups flaked coconut
1 teaspoon almond extract	1 (9-ounce) package milk
1 tablespoon orange juice	chocolate kisses (about 54)

In mixing bowl, cream butter, cream cheese, and sugar until light and fluffy. Add yolk, almond extract, and orange juice. Beat well. Combine flour, baking powder, and salt. Gradually add to creamed mixture until blended. Stir in 2 cups coconut. Cover dough and chill about 1 hour. Shape dough into 1-inch balls and roll in remaining coconut. Place on ungreased cookie sheet. Bake at 350 degrees for 10 to 12 minutes or until lightly browned on bottom. Remove from oven and immediately press kiss in center. Cool 1 minute and remove from cookie sheet. Yield: 4½ dozen.

Turtle Cookies

10	tablespoons butter	½	teaspoon baking soda
⅔	cup light brown sugar	2½	cups pecan halves
1	egg	20	marshmallows, cut in half
1	teaspoon vanilla		horizontally
¼	teaspoon salt	1	(6-ounce) package semi-sweet
1¾	cups flour		chocolate chips
½	teaspoon baking powder		

In mixing bowl, cream butter and sugar until light and fluffy. Beat in egg and vanilla. Add salt, flour, baking powder, and baking soda, mixing until blended. Refrigerate dough until ready to use. Place four pecan halves in clusters on parchment-lined or greased baking sheets. Break off small pieces of dough and roll into 1-inch balls. Place a ball in the center of each of the four pecans. Lightly press dough into pecans. Bake at 325 degrees for 10 to 15 minutes, or until bottoms are lightly browned. Remove from oven. Top each cookie with a marshmallow half, cut side down. Return to oven for 1 minute. Immediately press marshmallow down lightly. Remove to racks to cool. Melt chocolate in top of double boiler or microwave. Cover cookies with chocolate to cover the marshmallow. Cool until chocolate has hardened. May be refrigerated or stored in airtight container in cool place. Yield: Approximately 3 dozen turtle cookies.

NOTE: The kids will love these, but save some for the adults.

Pecan Pie Tarts

Crust:

1 (3-ounce) package cream cheese, softened	½ cup butter, softened
	1 cup flour

Mix cream cheese and butter with flour, mixing until the dough is smooth. Shape dough into a ball and refrigerate at least 1 hour. Press dough (1 tablespoon) into ungreased miniature muffin cups. Fill each pastry with pecans and Filling (see recipe below). Bake at 325 degrees for 20 to 25 minutes. Filling will puff and top will begin to crack when done.

Filling:

1 egg	Dash salt
¾ cup light brown sugar	1 teaspoon vanilla
1 tablespoon butter	¾ cup chopped pecans

In mixing bowl, beat egg, brown sugar, butter, salt, and vanilla until smooth. Divide pecans into two containers. Add egg mixture to half of pecans and pour mixture into pastry lined cups. Top filled cups with remaining pecans and bake as directed above. Yield: 2 dozen miniature pecan tarts.

Pecan Cups

2⅔ cups graham cracker crumbs	1 cup light brown sugar
1 (12-ounce) can evaporated milk	1½ cups chopped pecans
½ cup butter	1 cup flaked coconut

In mixing bowl, combine all ingredients together, blending well. Pour batter into lightly greased miniature muffin cups. Bake at 350 degrees for 10 to 12 minutes. Yield: 5 to 6 dozen cups.

NOTE: Great to make when in a pinch—easy and different.

Brandy Balls

1 (6-ounce) package semi-sweet chocolate chips
3 tablespoons light corn syrup
½ cup brandy
2½ cups finely chopped vanilla wafers

¾ cup finely chopped pecans
¼ cup powdered sugar
Powdered sugar for rolling

Melt chocolate over low heat in double boiler or in microwave. Remove from heat and add corn syrup and brandy. Combine vanilla wafers, pecans, and powdered sugar. Add chocolate mixture and mix well. Let stand 30 minutes. Form into small balls and roll in powdered or granulated sugar. Yield: 4 dozen.

Fruit Cake Bonbons

½ cup molasses
¼ cup water
1 (15-ounce) package raisins
1 (1-pound) jar mixed fruit
½ cup butter
⅔ cup sugar

3 eggs
1¼ cups flour
⅛ teaspoon baking soda
½ teaspoon cinnamon
½ cup orange juice
1 cup chopped pecans

Blend together molasses and water in a large, deep saucepan. Place over low heat. Stir until mixture comes to a boil. Add raisins, bring to a boil again and simmer for 5 minutes. Remove from heat, stir in mixed fruit. In mixing bowl, cream together butter and sugar. Blend in eggs, one at a time. Sift together flour, baking soda, and cinnamon. Add to butter mixture. Add orange juice. Then add molasses and fruit mixture and chopped pecans. Blend. Spoon mixture in miniature lined cupcake pans. Fill to top. Bake at 325 degrees for 20 to 25 minutes. Cool completely before storing. Yield: Approximately 8 dozen bonbons.

NOTE: Good for holiday season—use for parties.

Strudel

Dough:

3	cups flour	¼	cup lukewarm kosher grape wine
4	tablespoons sugar		Oil
½	teaspoon salt		Cinnamon and sugar
2	eggs		Graham cracker crumbs
⅔	cup corn oil		

In a mixing bowl, combine flour, sugar, and salt. Add eggs, oil, and wine, beating well. Cover with towel and let stand until Filling (see recipe below) is made. Knead dough after Filling is ready; take enough dough to form a ball the size of a baseball. Knead. Roll out on floured surface into a paper thin rectangle approximately 12 to 14 inches long. (Dough is stretchy and easy to work with). Fill three small bowls with oil, cinnamon and sugar mixture, and graham cracker crumbs so will have available. With pastry brush, brush dough with oil. Sprinkle with cinnamon and sugar and graham cracker crumbs. Spoon Filling in a roll along one end of length of rectangle. Roll dough up, tucking in ends as rolling. Carefully place roll on over-well oiled 15 × 10 × 2-inch jelly roll pan. Place 2 rolls on each pan. Brush roll with oil and then cut halfway through at diagonal about 1½ inches wide. Sprinkle with cinnamon and sugar mixture. Bake at 350 degrees for 1 hour or until strudel roll is brown. Baste with oil after baking 30 minutes. Remove from oven and slice where marks were cut. Repeat process until all dough is used. Yield: Approximately 100 pieces.

Filling:

2	cups mixed preserves (apricot, raspberry, and strawberry)	1	cup chopped pecans
		½	cup sugar
3	to 4 tart apples, peeled, cored, and grated, squeezing out all liquid	4	tablespoons kosher grape wine
		1	cup raisins
		1	large lemon, squeezed
1	cup flaked coconut		Graham cracker crumbs

In a large bowl, combine all ingredients except graham cracker crumbs, stirring well with wooden spoon. Add enough graham cracker crumbs to hold mixture together.

NOTE: This is my favorite Ft. Worth recipe that my mother's friends have graciously taught me how to make. It is a lot of work, but there is no strudel that even comes close to it — it is fantastic. Also, the ingredients are as close to exact as I can get them. Try it.

Chocolate Chip Mandel Bread

4	eggs	2	teaspoons baking powder
1	cup sugar	1	(6-ounce) package semi-sweet
1	cup oil		chocolate chips
1	teaspoon vanilla	1	cup chopped pecans
1	teaspoon lemon juice		Powdered sugar
4	cups flour		Cinnamon

In large mixing bowl, mix together eggs, sugar, oil, vanilla, and lemon juice. Sift flour and baking powder and add half of it to egg mixture. Add chocolate chips and pecans, mixing well. Add remaining flour, mixing until well combined. Form into 6 rolls 2 inches wide. Lay on greased cookie sheets and bake at 350 degrees for 20 to 25 minutes. Slice into 1-inch slices and roll into powdered sugar and cinnamon that has been combined together. Lower oven to 300 degrees and put slices standing up on cookie sheet and bake until dry. Yield: 6 to 7 dozen pieces.

White Chocolate Brownies with Chocolate Chunks

1	cup butter	½	cup sugar
10	ounces high quality white	1½	teaspoons vanilla
	chocolate, very finely chopped	2	cups flour
4	eggs	1	cup semi-sweet chocolate chunks
	Pinch of salt	1	cup chopped walnuts

In a small heavy saucepan over low heat, place the butter. When it has melted, remove the pan from the heat and add half of the white chocolate; *do not stir*. Let the mixture sit until needed. In a large mixing bowl, combine the eggs and the salt. Beat at high speed for about 30 seconds until frothy. Gradually add the sugar and continue to beat for 2 to 3 minutes until light in color. Add the white chocolate/butter mixture, vanilla, and flour. Quickly beat just until smooth. Stir in the remaining white chocolate and the semi-sweet chocolate chunks. Pour the batter into a greased and floured 13×9×2-inch baking pan, smoothing the top with a spatula. Bake for 30 to 35 minutes. Do not overcook. Leave the brownies in the pan and cool on a rack for 4 hours. Brownies will harden as cool.

NOTE: What can be better — white chocolate and semi-sweet?

Old Fashioned Brownies

1 cup butter	4 eggs
4 (1-ounce) squares unsweetened	Dash salt
chocolate	2 teaspoons vanilla
3 tablespoons light corn syrup	1 cup flour
1 cup light brown sugar	2 cups chopped pecans
1½ cups sugar	

In large heavy saucepan, combine butter, chocolate, and corn syrup, stirring until melted. Add sugars, mixing well. Remove from heat and add eggs, one at a time, beating well after each addition. Add salt, vanilla, and flour, stirring until mixed. Add pecans. Pour batter into a greased and floured 13×9×2-inch baking pan. Bake at 350 degrees for 30 minutes. Cool and ice with Chocolate Icing (see recipe below).

Chocolate Icing:

2 (1-ounce) squares unsweetened	Dash salt
chocolate	⅓ cup half-and-half cream
¼ cup butter	2 teaspoons vanilla
1 (16-ounce) box powdered sugar	

In top of double boiler or in microwave, melt chocolate and butter. Add sugar and salt, beating well. Add half-and-half to make icing spreading consistency. Add vanilla. Mix well and spread on cooled brownies.

Ultimate Brownie

1 cup butter, melted	1¼ cups sugar
5 (1-ounce) squares semi-sweet	1½ teaspoons baking powder
chocolate, melted	½ cup flour
2 (1-ounce) squares unsweetened	½ teaspoon salt
chocolate, melted	1 cup semi-sweet chocolate chips
3 eggs	1 cup chopped walnuts
1 tablespoon vanilla	

In large bowl, combine all ingredients and mix well. Pour into a greased and floured 13×9×2-inch baking pan. Bake at 350 degrees for 30 minutes.

NOTE: The name says it all!

Three Layer Brownies

1 **cup butter**	1 **cup flour**
¾ **cup cocoa**	1 **tablespoon vanilla**
2 **cups sugar**	1 **cup chopped pecans**
3 **eggs, well beaten**	

Melt butter in top of double boiler or microwave. Add cocoa and remove from heat. Add sugar and beaten eggs. Stir quickly until well mixed. Stir in flour, vanilla, and pecans. Pour batter into a greased and floured 13×9×2-inch baking pan. Bake at 325 degrees for 30 to 35 minutes. Do not overcook. Cool and ice with Icing (see recipe below).

Icing:

½ **cup butter, room temperature**	½ **teaspoon almond extract**
1 **(3-ounce) package cream cheese,**	½ **teaspoon vanilla**
room temperature	1 **to 2 tablespoons milk**
1 **(16-ounce) box powdered sugar**	

In mixing bowl, cream butter and cream cheese together. Add powdered sugar and flavorings. Add enough milk to make smooth and spreading consistency. Spread over cooled brownies and spread with Topping (see recipe below).

Topping:

3 **tablespoons butter**	2 **tablespoons sugar**
1 **(1-ounce) square unsweetened**	1½ **tablespoons Amaretto**
chocolate	
2 **(1-ounce) squares semi-sweet**	
chocolate	

Melt butter and chocolate in top of double boiler or microwave. Remove from heat. Add sugar and Amaretto. Mix well. Spread over Icing. Refrigerate until firm.

Heavenly Hash

½ cup butter	1 teaspoon baking powder
1 cup sugar	1 teaspoon vanilla
4 eggs	1 (10½-ounce) package miniature
1 (16-ounce) can chocolate syrup	marshmallows
1 cup flour	1 cup chopped pecans, toasted

In large mixing bowl, cream butter and sugar. Add eggs and beat well. Gradually add chocolate syrup. Combine flour and baking powder and add to sugar mixture, blending well. Add vanilla. Pour batter into a greased and floured $13 \times 9 \times 2$-inch baking pan. Bake at 350 degrees for 30 minutes. When cake is done, remove from oven and immediately cover with miniature marshmallows and toasted pecans. Spread with Chocolate Frosting (see recipe below).

Chocolate Frosting:

3 (1-ounce) squares unsweetened	1 teaspoon vanilla
chocolate	1 (16-ounce) box powdered sugar
½ cup plus 2 tablespoons butter	2 to 3 tablespoons milk
1 egg	

In top of double boiler or microwave, melt chocolate and butter. Set aside to cool. Add egg, beating well. Add vanilla and powdered sugar. Add enough milk to make frosting spreading consistency. Pour Frosting on top of marshmallows. If desired, sprinkle with more pecans.

NOTE: One of the best Heavenly Hash recipes I've found.

Deluxe Chocolate Rocky Road Bars

Crust:

½ cup butter
1 (1-ounce) square unsweetened
   chocolate
1 cup flour
1 teaspoon baking powder

2 eggs
1 cup sugar
1 teaspoon vanilla
1 cup chopped pecans

Melt butter and chocolate in top of double boiler or in microwave; cool. Sift together flour and baking powder, set aside. In medium bowl, beat eggs, sugar, and vanilla. Add chocolate mixture, beating well. Add flour mixture and pecans. Spread in a greased and floured 13 × 9 × 2-inch baking pan and top with Filling (see recipe below).

Filling:

6 ounces cream cheese, softened
4 tablespoons butter, softened
½ cup sugar
1 egg
½ teaspoon vanilla

2 tablespoons flour
¼ cup chopped pecans
1 (6-ounce) package semi-sweet
   chocolate chips
3 cups miniature marshmallows

In mixing bowl, beat together cream cheese, butter, and sugar until fluffy. Add egg, vanilla, and flour. Beat well. Stir in pecans and spread batter over unbaked crust. Sprinkle with chocolate chips. Bake at 350 degrees for 30 to 35 minutes. Remove from oven and sprinkle with marshmallows. Return to oven for 2 minutes. Spread with Frosting (see recipe below).

Frosting:

4 tablespoons butter
1 (1-ounce) square unsweetened
   chocolate
2 ounces cream cheese

¼ cup milk
1 teaspoon vanilla
3 cups powdered sugar

Melt together butter and chocolate in top of double boiler or microwave; cool. Add cream cheese, milk, vanilla, and powdered sugar, beating until smooth. Spread over marshmallow layer. Cool and cut into bars.

NOTE: Yummy!

Colorful Blonde Brownies

1   (16-ounce) box light brown
    sugar
1¼ cups flour
1   teaspoon baking powder
2   eggs
1   cup butter, melted

Dash salt
1   teaspoon vanilla
1   cup chopped pecans
1   cup candy-coated milk chocolate
    candies

In bowl, combine sugar, flour, and baking powder. Add dry ingredients to eggs and add other ingredients, mixing well. Pour batter into a greased and floured 13×9×2-inch baking pan. Bake at 300 degrees for 45 minutes or until batter falls. Do not overcook. Let cool and cut into squares.

NOTE: This will definitely be a kid's favorite.

Pecan Toffee Bars

1½ cups flour
⅓   cup powdered sugar
¾   cup butter, cut into pieces
1   (14-ounce) can sweetened
    condensed milk
1   egg, beaten

1   teaspoon vanilla
1   cup chopped pecans
6   (1³/₁₆-ounce) English toffee
    candy bars, cut into ¼-inch
    pieces

In medium bowl, combine flour and sugar. Cut in butter until mixture resembles coarse meal. Press firmly into bottom of 13×9×2-inch baking pan. Bake at 350 degrees for 15 minutes, or until lightly golden and edges begin to darken. In medium bowl, combine milk, egg, and vanilla. Stir in pecans and English toffee. Pour into partially baked crust. Bake at 350 degrees for another 20 to 23 minutes, or until golden brown. Cool. Refrigerate. Cut into bars.

Chocolate Almond Squares

½ cup butter, room temperature
½ cup light brown sugar
1   teaspoon vanilla

¼   teaspoon salt
1½ cups flour
¾   cup seedless raspberry jam

In mixing bowl, combine all ingredients except jam. Mix until smooth. Pat dough into 13×9×2-inch baking pan. Bake at 350 degrees for 15 minutes until golden. Spread with jam and top with Almond Layer (see recipe below). Continue baking for 20 minutes or until golden. Cool and ice with Chocolate Icing (see recipe below).

Almond Layer:

3 eggs
8 ounces almond paste
½ cup sugar

1 cup blanched almonds, toasted
   and ground
1 teaspoon almond extract

In mixing bowl, combine all ingredients and mix until smooth. Pour over cookie layer and bake 20 minutes or until golden.

Chocolate Icing:

1 (1-ounce) square unsweetened
   chocolate
2 tablespoons butter, room
   temperature

1½ cups powdered sugar
2   tablespoons light cream
1   tablespoon coffee liqueur
    (optional)

Melt chocolate in small saucepan over low heat or in microwave. Add butter, sugar, cream, and liqueur. Blend well. Spread over baked cookies.

NOTE: Raspberry, almond, and chocolate make this an extra special bar cookie.

Chocolate Candy Bars

½   cup butter, softened
1¼ cups sugar
3   eggs
3   tablespoons plus 1 teaspoon
    cocoa

1   cup flour
½   cup chopped walnuts
1   (14-ounce) can sweetened
    condensed milk
2   cups flaked coconut

In large bowl, cream butter and sugar until light. Beat in eggs. Stir in cocoa, flour, and walnuts. Mix well. Spread batter into a greased and floured 13×9×2-inch baking pan. Bake at 350 degrees for 20 minutes. In small bowl, mix condensed milk and coconut. Spread on top of crust and bake an additional 18 to 20 minutes. Frost immediately with Chocolate Frosting (see recipe below).

Chocolate Frosting:

1   (1-ounce) square unsweetened
    chocolate
1   tablespoon butter

2   cups powdered sugar
2   tablespoons milk
1   teaspoon vanilla

In top of double boiler or in microwave, melt chocolate and butter, stirring until smooth. Add powdered sugar, milk, and vanilla. Beat until ingredients are well mixed and spread on top. Cool and cut into squares.

Chocolate Crunch Bars

1   cup butter
1½ cups sugar
2   egg yolks
2½ cups flour
1   (6-ounce) package semi-sweet
    chocolate chips

4   egg whites
¼   teaspoon salt
2   cups finely chopped pecans

In mixing bowl, cream the butter and ½ cup sugar with the egg yolks. Add flour. Pat batter into a greased 15×10×1-inch baking sheet about ⅜-inch thick. Bake at 350 degrees for 15 minutes. Remove from oven and top with chocolate chips. In another bowl, beat egg whites with salt until stiff. Fold in remaining 1 cup sugar and pecans. Gently spread on top of chocolate. Bake at 350 degrees for 25 minutes.

Chocolate Raisin-Peanut Bars

1   cup sugar
1   cup butter, softened
¼   cup dark corn syrup
1   teaspoon vanilla
1   egg yolk
2   cups flour

1   cup raisins
1   cup salted peanuts
⅓   cup creamy peanut butter
1   (12-ounce) package semi-sweet
    chocolate chips

In a 2½-quart bowl, mix sugar, butter, corn syrup, vanilla, and egg yolk. Stir in flour. Press dough in an ungreased 13×9×2-inch baking pan. Bake at 350 degrees for 20 to 25 minutes, or until golden brown. In a saucepan, mix raisins, peanuts, peanut butter, and chocolate chips. Heat over low heat, stirring constantly, until chocolate chips are melted. Spread over crust in pan. Refrigerate at least 2 hours.

NOTE: Do not let these ingredients fool you — this is a delicious bar cookie.

Peanut Butter Squares

½ cup butter, softened
½ cup sugar
½ cup light brown sugar
1 egg
⅓ cup crunchy peanut butter

1 cup flour
½ teaspoon baking soda
¼ teaspoon salt
1 cup old fashioned oatmeal

In large mixing bowl, combine butter, sugars, egg, and peanut butter until well mixed. In small bowl, combine flour, baking soda, and salt. Stir in flour mixture and oatmeal. Spread in a greased and floured 13×9×2-inch baking pan and bake at 350 degrees for 15 minutes. Cool. Frost with Chocolate Peanut Butter Frosting (see recipe below). Yield: 4 dozen squares.

Chocolate Peanut Butter Frosting:

1½ cups powdered sugar
¼ cup crunchy peanut butter
3 tablespoons milk

3 tablespoons cocoa
1 tablespoon milk

In small bowl, mix powdered sugar, peanut butter, and 3 tablespoons milk until creamy. Add additional milk until spreading consistency. Reserve ⅓ cup frosting. Add cocoa and 1 tablespoon milk to remaining frosting. Frost with the Chocolate Peanut Butter Frosting and drop Peanut Butter Frosting by teaspoonfuls onto top of cake with Chocolate Peanut Butter Frosting. Swirl frostings for marbled effect. Yield: 4 dozen squares.

Pecan Pie Bars

2 cups flour
⅔ cup powdered sugar

1 cup butter, softened

Combine flour and powdered sugar. Cut in butter and pat into 13×9×2-inch baking pan. Bake at 350 degrees for 20 minutes. Pour Pecan Pie Filling (see recipe below) over hot pastry and continue baking for 25 minutes more.

Pecan Pie Filling:

⅔ cup butter, melted
½ cup light brown sugar
½ cup honey

3 tablespoons whipping cream
2½ cups coarsely chopped pecans

Combine all ingredients together and pour over hot pastry. Continue baking as directed.

NOTE: This is one of the best bar cookies you will ever have.

Graham Cracker Dream Squares

1½ cups graham cracker crumbs
¼ cup light brown sugar
6 tablespoons butter, melted
1 (12-ounce) package semi-sweet chocolate chips
1 cup flaked coconut

1 cup chopped pecans
1 (7-ounce) jar marshmallow creme
2 tablespoons milk
1 teaspoon vanilla

In bowl, combine crumbs, brown sugar, and butter. Press into a 13×9×2-inch baking pan. Bake at 350 degrees for 10 minutes; remove from oven. In small bowl, combine chocolate chips, coconut, and pecans. Sprinkle evenly over first layer. Thin marshmallow creme with milk and vanilla. Drizzle over top. Return to oven and bake another 15 minutes. Cool before cutting into squares. Yield: 4 to 5 dozen.

NOTE: So simple and so good!

Chess Bars

¾ cup butter
1½ cups flour
3   tablespoons sugar
1   (16-ounce) box light brown
    sugar

4   egg yolks, beaten
1   cup coarsely chopped pecans
1   teaspoon vanilla
4   egg whites

Cream butter; add flour and sugar. Pat into a 13×9×2-inch baking pan. Bake at 375 degrees for 20 to 30 minutes or until crust is golden brown. Meanwhile, make filling by mixing the brown sugar with beaten egg yolks. When thick and spongy, add pecans. Add vanilla. Beat egg whites until stiff peaks form and fold into brown sugar mixture. Spread filling evenly over the partially baked crust. Return to oven and bake 25 to 30 minutes longer, or until the filling sets. Filling should be transparent and semi-soft, never hard or chewy. Cool and cut into squares.

Ooey Gooey Squares

1   (18½-ounce) box butter cake
    mix
1   egg
½ cup butter, melted
1   (8-ounce) package cream cheese
1   (16-ounce) box powdered sugar

2   eggs, beaten
1   teaspoon vanilla
1   cup flaked coconut
1   cup chopped pecans
1   (6-ounce) package semi-sweet
    chocolate chips

In bowl, combine cake mix, 1 egg and butter and pat into the bottom of a 13×9×2-inch baking pan. In mixing bowl, blend cream cheese and powdered sugar. Add 2 beaten eggs and mix well. Add vanilla. Stir in coconut, pecans, and chocolate chips. Pour mixture on top of bottom layer in pan. Bake at 350 degrees for 45 minutes. Cool and cut into squares.

NOTE: These bar cookies are irresistible and will disappear very quickly.

Cream Cheese Butter Bars

1 cup butter, softened	2 cups self-rising flour
1 cup sugar	1 cup chopped pecans
1 teaspoon vanilla	

In large mixing bowl, cream butter and sugar until light and fluffy. Add vanilla. Gradually add flour, mixing well. Add pecans. Pat dough evenly over bottom of an ungreased 15 × 10 × 1-inch jelly roll pan. Bake at 350 degrees for 15 to 20 minutes or until lightly browned. Spread crust with Cream Cheese Topping (see recipe below). Continue to bake for 30 to 35 minutes. Cool completely. Cut into diamonds or squares. Yield: 4 to 5 dozen.

Cream Cheese Topping:

2 (8-ounce) packages cream cheese, softened	1 teaspoon vanilla
	2 cups powdered sugar
2 eggs	1 cup sour cream

In large mixing bowl, beat cream cheese until smooth. Add eggs and vanilla, beating until smooth. Gradually add powdered sugar; mixing well. Fold in sour cream. Pour over partially baked crust.

NOTE: Place cherry topping on each square to make it look pretty, if desired. These are delicious.

Coconut Butter Bars

¾ cup butter	1 (3-ounce) package cream cheese
½ cup sugar	¼ cup butter
2 cups flour	¾ cup light brown sugar
½ teaspoon salt	1 cup flaked coconut
1 teaspoon vanilla	

In bowl, mix butter, sugar, flour, salt, and vanilla until well blended. Press all but 1 cup firmly into bottom of an ungreased 13 × 9 × 2-inch baking pan. In mixing bowl, combine cream cheese, butter, brown sugar, and coconut, beating well. Drop by spoonfuls over butter/flour mixture in pan and bake at 350 degrees for 5 minutes. Smooth this mixture over crust. Sprinkle with remaining topping. Continue baking for 25 to 30 minutes, or until light golden brown. Yield: Approximately 5 dozen.

Lemon Nut Chess Bars

2   cups flour   1   cup butter
½   cup powdered sugar

Combine flour and powdered sugar. Cut in butter and pat into 13×9×2-inch baking pan. Bake at 350 degrees for 15 minutes. Pour Lemon Filling (see recipe below) over hot pastry and continue baking for 25 to 30 minutes more or until filling is set. After cake is done, spread with Lemon Glaze (see recipe below) while hot, if desired. Cool and cut into bars. Yield: 3 to 4 dozen bars.

Lemon Filling:

4   eggs, beaten   ¼   cup flour
2   cups sugar   ½   teaspoon baking powder
½   cup fresh lemon juice   1   cup chopped pecans
1   teaspoon grated lemon rind

In mixing bowl, combine eggs and sugar and beat until light in color. Add lemon juice and rind, mixing well. Combine flour and baking powder and add to creamed mixture. Stir in pecans. Pour into hot pastry and continue baking as directed.

Lemon Glaze:

1   tablespoon butter   Lemon juice to make spreading
1   cup powdered sugar   consistency

Combine butter and powdered sugar. Gradually add lemon juice until spreading consistency is reached. Spread gently over cake while hot.

NOTE: These are always guaranteed to be a hit.

Lemon Crumb Squares

1 (14-ounce) can sweetened condensed milk	1 teaspoon baking powder
½ cup lemon juice	½ teaspoon salt
1 teaspoon grated lemon rind	¾ cup butter
1½ cups flour	1¼ cups light brown sugar
	1½ cups old fashioned oatmeal

Combine milk, juice, and lemon rind. Set aside. Sift flour, baking powder, and salt. In mixing bowl, cream butter and sugar until light and fluffy. Add oatmeal and flour mixture and mix until crumbly. Spread half mixture in 12 × 8 × 2-inch buttered pan and pat down crust. Spread milk mixture over top and cover with remaining crumb mixture. Bake at 350 degrees for 25 minutes or until edges turn brown. Cool in pan about 15 minutes; cut.

NOTE: These are best when served day made.

Fresh Citrus Blonde Brownies

1¼ cups flour	1 teaspoon vanilla
1¼ teaspoons baking powder	1 tablespoon grated orange rind
½ teaspoon salt	1 teaspoon grated lemon rind
⅔ cup butter, softened	2 eggs
½ cup sugar	2 teaspoons orange juice
⅔ cup light brown sugar	½ cup slivered almonds

Combine flour, baking powder, and salt in small bowl. Set aside. In mixing bowl, beat together butter, sugar, and brown sugar until light and fluffy. Add vanilla and orange and lemon rinds, mix well. Beat in eggs, one at a time, beating well after each addition. Blend in orange juice. Fold in flour mixture and almonds. Spread in a greased and floured 9 × 9 × 2-inch baking pan. Bake at 350 degrees for 30 to 35 minutes or until toothpick comes out barely moist. Cool and ice with Orange Glaze (see recipe below).

Orange Glaze:

2 tablespoons butter, softened	1 tablespoon milk
½ cup powdered sugar	1 teaspoon grated orange rind
2 teaspoons orange juice	

In bowl, combine all ingredients and beat until smooth and creamy. Ice cool cake.

Marmalade Bars

1 cup orange marmalade	½ cup butter
½ cup chopped pecans	1 cup light brown sugar
½ cup flaked coconut	1 egg
1½ cups flour	2 tablespoons orange juice
1 teaspoon baking powder	1½ cups old fashioned oatmeal
¼ teaspoon baking soda	1 teaspoon vanilla
¼ teaspoon salt	

In bowl, combine marmalade, pecans, and coconut; set aside. Combine flour, baking powder, baking soda, and salt. In mixing bowl, cream butter and sugar, beating until light and fluffy. Add egg and orange juice; beat well. Stir in oatmeal and dry ingredients. Spread half batter in a greased and floured 13 × 9 × 2-inch baking pan. Cover with orange-pecan mixture. Drop remaining batter by teaspoons over filling. Spread carefully. Bake at 350 degrees for 30 to 35 minutes or until golden brown. Frost with Icing (see recipe below).

Icing:

2 tablespoons butter, softened	1 teaspoon grated orange rind
1½ cups powdered sugar	2 to 3 tablespoons orange juice

In small bowl, combine all ingredients except orange juice. Add enough orange juice until mixture is spreading consistency.

Apricot Bars

1 cup dried apricots, finely chopped	2 eggs
Boiling water	1 tablespoon apricot brandy
½ cup unsalted butter, room temperature	1 teaspoon grated orange rind
	1½ cups flour
2 cups light brown sugar	1 teaspoon baking powder
	½ teaspoon salt

Place dried apricots in bowl and cover with boiling water. Soak 10 to 15 minutes, then drain well. In mixing bowl, cream butter and sugar until light and fluffy. Add eggs, brandy, and orange rind. Mix well. Combine flour, baking powder, and salt and add to creamed mixture. Fold in apricots. Pour batter into a greased and floured 15×10×1-inch jelly roll pan. Bake at 350 degrees for 20 to 25 minutes or until tester comes clean. Remove cake from oven and cool 10 minutes. Spread Icing (see recipe below) to cover.

Icing:

3 cups powdered sugar	3 teaspoons lemon juice
3 tablespoons butter, softened	1½ teaspoons grated orange rind
3 teaspoons fresh orange juice	½ cup finely chopped pecans

Blend all ingredients except pecans in small bowl until creamy. Spread icing over cake. Sprinkle with pecans and press lightly. Cut into bars.

NOTE: You can get a lot of bar cookies from this tasty recipe.

Three Layer Meltaways

2	cups graham cracker crumbs	1	egg, beaten
1	cup flaked coconut	½	cup butter, melted
¾	cup chopped pecans	1	(1-ounce) square unsweetened
1	teaspoon vanilla		chocolate, melted
¼	cup sugar		

Mix together all ingredients and press into a $9 \times 9 \times 2$-inch square baking pan. Chill and spread with Filling (see recipe below).

Filling:

2	cups powdered sugar	1	tablespoon milk
1	teaspoon vanilla	¼	cup butter, melted

In mixing bowl, beat all ingredients together and spread over chilled crust. Refrigerate until filling sets and top with Glaze (see recipe below).

Glaze:

2   (1-ounce) squares unsweetened
    chocolate

In top of double boiler or microwave, melt chocolate. Pour over filling and spread carefully. Chill.

Creme de Menthe Squares

½ cup butter	1 egg, beaten
½ cup cocoa	1 teaspoon vanilla
½ cup powdered sugar	2 cups graham cracker crumbs

Combine ½ cup butter and cocoa in saucepan over low heat. Stir until blended. Remove from heat and add ½ cup powdered sugar, egg, and vanilla. Stir in graham cracker crumbs and mix well. Press into bottom of an ungreased 13×9×2-inch baking pan. Top with Middle Layer (see recipe below).

Middle Layer:

½ cup butter, melted	3 cups powdered sugar
⅓ cup creme de menthe	

In mixing bowl, beat butter and creme de menthe. Add powdered sugar, mixing until smooth. Spread over chocolate layer. Chill 1 hour in refrigerator and top with Chocolate Glaze (see recipe below).

Chocolate Glaze:

¼ cup butter	1½ cups semi-sweet chocolate chips

In microwave or in saucepan, combine ¼ cup butter and chocolate pieces and cook over low heat until melted. Spread over middle layer. Chill 1 to 2 hours in refrigerator.

NOTE: Freezes well and tastes great frozen.

Chocolate Thins

½ cup butter
1 (1-ounce) square unsweetened
   chocolate
¼ cup sugar
1 teaspoon vanilla

1 egg, beaten
1 cup graham cracker crumbs
1 cup old fashioned oatmeal
1 cup finely chopped pecans

In microwave or in top of double boiler, melt butter and chocolate. In mixing bowl, blend sugar, vanilla, egg, graham cracker crumbs, oatmeal, and pecans together. Add melted chocolate mixture. Mix until dough comes together. Press mixture into a 13×9×2-inch baking pan. Refrigerate while making Filling (see recipe below).

Filling:

4 tablespoons butter
2 cups powdered sugar

1½ tablespoons Grand Marnier
1 tablespoon milk

In mixing bowl, beat butter, powdered sugar, Grand Marnier, and milk. Spread over chocolate crumb mixture. Refrigerate while making Glaze (see recipe below).

Glaze:

4 (1-ounce) squares unsweetened
   chocolate

In microwave or top of double boiler, melt chocolate. Spread over filling. Refrigerate. Cut into squares before chocolate hardens. Store in refrigerator indefinitely.

NOTE: A light delicious after dinner cookie.

Mock Strudel

2¼ cups flour	1 cup sour cream
1 tablespoon sugar	1 (16-ounce) jar apricot preserves
½ teaspoon salt	Powdered sugar for sprinkling
1 cup butter, melted	

Combine all ingredients except apricot preserves and powdered sugar in a bowl and stir until mixture forms a ball. Wrap dough in waxed paper and refrigerate for 1 hour. Remove from refrigerator and divide into four equal parts. Roll each piece of dough out on floured waxed paper to form a rectangle. Spread apricot preserves over entire rectangle. Sprinkle Filling (see recipe below) over preserves. Roll each rectangle up lengthwise to form a roll. Place roll on greased and floured baking sheet. Repeat with remaining dough. Bake at 350 degrees for 1 hour. Sprinkle with powdered sugar. Let cool and slice into 1-inch slices.

Filling

½ cup light brown sugar	1 cup chopped walnuts
1 tablespoon cinnamon	½ cup white raisins

Combine all ingredients in a bowl, mixing well.

NOTE: Strudel is always a treat to eat, and this recipe makes it possible for anyone to prepare.

Cakes

Old Fashioned Sour Cream Coffee Cake

½	cup butter	1	teaspoon baking powder
1	cup sugar	1	teaspoon baking soda
3	eggs	1	cup sour cream
2	cups flour	1	teaspoon vanilla

In large mixing bowl, cream butter and sugar until well combined. Add eggs, one at a time, beating well after each addition. Combine dry ingredients and add alternately with sour cream, beginning and ending with flour mixture. Add vanilla and mix well. Pour half of batter into a greased and floured angel food pan. Sprinkle with half of Praline Mix (see recipe below). Top with remaining batter and remaining Praline Mix. Bake at 350 degrees for 40 to 45 minutes. Cool 20 minutes. Remove from pan.

Praline Mix:

1	cup light brown sugar	⅓	cup butter, softened
2	teaspoons cinnamon	¾	cup chopped pecans

In small bowl, combine brown sugar and cinnamon. Cut in butter with pastry blender until mixture is crumbly. Add pecans.

Cream Cheese Pound Cake

1½	cups butter, softened	6	eggs
1	(8-ounce) package cream cheese, softened	3	cups flour
		1	teaspoon vanilla
3	cups sugar		

In large mixing bowl, cream butter and cream cheese until well combined. Blend in sugar, 1 cup at a time, mixing well. Add eggs one at a time, beating well after each addition. Add flour and vanilla a little at a time, blending until smooth. Pour into a greased and floured tube pan. (Do not use a bundt pan). Bake at 325 degrees for 1 hour and 10 minutes. Cool in pan 10 to 15 minutes, then invert on platter.

Pound Cake

¾   cup butter
1   (16-ounce) box powdered sugar
6   eggs

2   cups flour
1   teaspoon vanilla
1   teaspoon almond extract

In mixing bowl, cream butter and sugar until light and fluffy. Add eggs one at a time, beating well after each addition. Gradually add flour, beating well. Add vanilla and almond extract. Bake in a greased and floured angel food pan at 325 degrees for 45 minutes to 1 hour.

Poppy Seed Cake

3   cups flour
½   teaspoon salt
1½   teaspoons baking powder
3   eggs
1¼   cups oil
2   cups sugar
1½   cups milk

1   tablespoon grated lemon rind
2   tablespoons poppy seeds
1   teaspoon almond extract
1   teaspoon butter flavoring
1   teaspoon vanilla
1   teaspoon lemon extract

Combine flour, salt, and baking powder together in bowl. Beat eggs, oil, and sugar together in mixing bowl. Add to flour mixture, mixing well. Add milk slowly. Stir in rind, poppy seeds, and flavorings. Pour into a greased and floured 10-inch bundt pan. Bake at 350 degrees for 50 to 60 minutes, or until top cracks. Cool 15 minutes and invert on serving plate. Drizzle with Glaze (see recipe below).

Glaze:

½   cup orange juice
1½   cups powdered sugar
1   teaspoon vanilla

1   teaspoon butter flavoring
½   teaspoon almond extract

Mix together and pour over hot cake.

Yam Pound Cake

1¼	cups oil	1	teaspoon salt
2	cups sugar	1½	teaspoons cinnamon
4	eggs	1	teaspoon nutmeg
2	teaspoons vanilla	1	(29-ounce) can cooked yams or
2	cups flour		2 cups cooked yams, mashed
1½	teaspoons baking soda	1	cup chopped pecans
½	teaspoon cloves	1	cup flaked coconut

In large bowl, combine oil and sugar, mixing well. Add eggs, one at a time, beating well after each addition. Add vanilla. Sift dry ingredients and add to creamed mixture. Add yams, pecans, and coconut. Bake in a greased and floured 10-inch bundt pan at 350 degrees for 1 hour and 5 minutes to 1 hour and 15 minutes. Invert onto cooling rack. When cake is cool, ice with Icing (see recipe below).

Icing:

¼	cup butter	½	(16-ounce) box powdered sugar
1	(3-ounce) package cream cheese	½	teaspoon vanilla

In large bowl, cream all ingredients together until well blended.

NOTE: This cake is very moist and delicious.

Apricot Brandy Pound Cake

1 cup butter	1 teaspoon orange extract
3 cups sugar	¼ teaspoon almond extract
6 eggs	½ teaspoon lemon extract
3 cups flour	1 teaspoon vanilla
¼ teaspoon baking soda	½ cup apricot brandy
½ teaspoon salt	Grated rind of orange
1 cup sour cream	

In mixing bowl, cream butter and sugar until light and fluffy. Add eggs, one at a time, beating thoroughly. Sift flour with baking soda and salt. In a separate bowl, combine sour cream, extracts, vanilla, and brandy. Add orange rind. Add flour and sour cream mixtures alternately to the butter/sugar mixture. Mix just until blended. Pour batter into a greased and floured 10-inch tube pan. Bake at 325 degrees for 1 hour to 1 hour and 10 minutes, or until cake tester comes out clean. Let stand 10 minutes and remove from pan. Spread with Glaze (see recipe below).

Glaze:

2 tablespoons orange juice	½ teaspoon grated lemon rind
2 tablespoons lemon juice	1 cup powdered sugar

Whisk together milk, lemon juice, lemon rind, and powdered sugar to desired consistency. Spread on cake.

Grand Marnier Pound Cake

1	cup butter	1	teaspoon baking soda
1	cup sugar	1	teaspoon baking powder
3	eggs, separated	1	cup sour cream
1	tablespoon Grand Marnier		Grated rind of 1 orange
2	cups flour	1	cup chopped walnuts

In large mixing bowl, cream butter and sugar until light and fluffy. Beat in egg yolks, one at a time, beating well after each addition. Add Grand Marnier. Sift dry ingredients together and add to creamed mixture alternately with sour cream, beginning and ending with dry ingredients. Mix until smooth. Stir in orange rind and walnuts. In small mixing bowl, beat egg whites until stiff and fold into batter. Pour batter into a greased and floured 10-inch fluted bundt pan. Bake at 350 degrees for 45 to 55 minutes. Remove cake from oven when done and allow to stand 5 minutes. Invert on cake plate. Prick the cake all over with a toothpick. Spoon cooled Syrup (see recipe below) over the top until all has been absorbed.

Syrup:

½	cup powdered sugar	¼	cup Grand Marnier
½	cup orange juice		

While cake is baking, mix together sugar and orange juice and heat in saucepan over medium heat, stirring only until sugar is dissolved. Allow to cool, then add Grand Marnier.

Orange Cranberry Cake

½	cup butter	¼	teaspoon salt
1	cup sugar	½	cup fresh orange juice
1	egg	½	cup milk
1	tablespoon grated orange rind	1	cup chopped walnuts
2¼	cups flour	1½	cups fresh cranberries
1	teaspoon baking soda	1	cup chopped dates

In mixing bowl, cream butter and sugar until light and fluffy. Add egg and orange rind, beating well. Combine flour, baking soda, and salt and add to creamed mixture alternately with orange juice and milk. Stir in walnuts, cranberries, and dates. Bake in greased and floured 10-inch bundt pan at 350 degrees for 1 hour. Invert to serving platter and pour over hot Glaze (see recipe below).

Glaze:

1½	cups powdered sugar	3	tablespoons orange juice

In saucepan, combine sugar and orange juice over low heat until well combined. Pour over hot cake.

Cranberry Cake with Hot Butter Sauce

2	tablespoons butter, melted	3	teaspoons baking powder
1	cup sugar	½	teaspoon salt
1	teaspoon vanilla	1	cup milk
2	cups cake flour	2	cups fresh cranberries

In a large mixing bowl, cream butter and sugar until light and fluffy. Add vanilla. In a separate bowl, sift together flour, baking powder, and salt. Add flour mixture and milk alternately to butter mixture and mix thoroughly. Fold in cranberries. Pour batter into a greased $9 \times 9 \times 2$-inch square baking pan. Bake at 400 degrees for 30 to 35 minutes. While cake is hot, cut into squares and top with Hot Butter Sauce (see recipe below).

Hot Butter Sauce:

½	cup butter	½	cup half-and-half cream
1	cup sugar		

In a medium saucepan, melt butter and blend in sugar. Stir in half-and-half and simmer 3 to 4 minutes, stirring occasionally.

Peach Nut Cake

2	cups sugar	1	cup buttermilk
1	cup butter	1	cup chopped pecans
3	eggs	2	cups flour
2	teaspoons baking soda	2	cups mashed peaches

In bowl, mix sugar and butter until light and fluffy. Add eggs, beating well. Dissolve baking soda in buttermilk. Dredge pecans in small amount of flour; add remaining flour to mixture alternately with buttermilk. Add peaches, well drained, and pecans. Pour into a greased and floured 10-inch tube pan. Bake at 350 degrees for 1 hour. Cool and invert onto serving dish. Drizzle Glaze (see recipe below) over top of cake.

Glaze:

½ to 1 cup powdered sugar		¼	cup peach or apricot brandy
2	tablespoons butter		

Combine all ingredients.

Plum Good Cake

2	cups flour	1	teaspoon cinnamon
2½	teaspoons baking powder	2	(4½-ounce) jars plums with
½	teaspoon salt		tapioca baby food
2	cups sugar	1	cup chopped pecans
3	eggs	¾	cup oil

In large bowl, mix all ingredients together. Do not use mixer. Pour batter into a greased and floured 10-inch bundt pan. Bake at 350 degrees for 50 minutes. Cool and frost with Foamy Icing (see recipe below).

Foamy Icing:

¼	cup butter	2	cups powdered sugar
¼	teaspoon salt	½	cup marshmallow creme
1	(3-ounce) package cream cheese		

In mixing bowl, beat all ingredients together until light and foamy. Frost cool cake.

NOTE: This cream cheese icing with this spicy cake is a good combination.

Luscious Lemon Layer Cake

3 cups flour	2 cups sugar
½ teaspoon salt	3 eggs, room temperature
½ teaspoon baking soda	1 cup buttermilk
1 cup unsalted butter, room	3 tablespoons fresh lemon juice
temperature	1 tablespoon grated lemon rind

Sift first 3 ingredients into medium bowl. In mixing bowl, cream butter with sugar until light and fluffy. Add eggs, one at a time, beating well after each addition. Mix in dry ingredients alternately with buttermilk, beginning and ending with dry ingredients. Mix in lemon juice and rind. Pour batter into a greased and floured 10-inch bundt pan and bake at 325 degrees for 50 to 60 minutes. Cool cake in pan on wire rack for 15 minutes. Meanwhile, prepare Glaze (see recipe below).

Glaze:

1 cup powdered sugar	2 tablespoons unsalted butter,
¼ cup fresh lemon juice	melted

Stir all ingredients in small bowl until smooth. Invert cake onto plate. Brush glaze over warm cake. Cool completely. Carefully split cooled cake in half horizontally and spread with Lemon Frosting (see recipe below).

Lemon Frosting:

3 tablespoons unsalted butter,	2½ cups powdered sugar
room temperature	2 tablespoons lemon juice
1 (3-ounce) package cream cheese,	1 teaspoon grated lemon rind
room temperature	

In mixing bowl, beat butter with cream cheese until light. Gradually beat in powdered sugar. Mix in lemon juice and lemon rind. Spread between layers and carefully replace top. Spread frosting over top and sides of cake, swirling Frosting.

NOTE: An incredible lemon cake.

Coconut Cream Cake

½ cup butter	2 teaspoons baking powder
½ cup sugar	⅛ teaspoon salt
4 egg yolks	¼ cup milk
1 cup flour	1 teaspoon vanilla

In large mixing bowl, cream butter and sugar until fluffy. Add egg yolks and mix well. Sift dry ingredients together. Combine milk and vanilla together in small measuring cup. Add dry ingredients alternately with milk mixture to sugar mixture until well combined. Pour into two greased and floured 8-inch round pans. Top with Meringue (see recipe below) and bake at 350 degrees for 20 to 30 minutes. Remove cake from pans and cool. Turn one layer meringue side up on serving plate. Spread with Coconut Cream Filling (see recipe below) and top with second layer, meringue side up.

Meringue:

4 egg whites	1 teaspoon vanilla
1 cup sugar	

In mixing bowl, beat egg whites until stiff and gradually beat in sugar. Fold in vanilla. Spread over batter in pans and bake as directed. Cool cake layers and remove from pans.

Coconut Cream Filling:

½ cup sugar	2 tablespoons butter
2 tablespoons flour	1½ teaspoons vanilla
2 egg yolks	½ (6-ounce) package frozen
1 (5⅓-ounce) can evaporated milk	coconut, thawed
2 tablespoons milk	

Combine sugar, flour, and egg yolks in saucepan. Add both milks to egg mixture, cooking until thick. Remove from heat and add butter and vanilla. Fold in grated coconut. Spread filling on top of meringue of bottom layer.

NOTE: This cake is unusual and delicious.

Piña Colada Cake

2 cups sugar	1 teaspoon coconut extract
1 cup butter, softened	1 tablespoon rum
4 eggs	3 cups flour
1 cup unsweetened pineapple juice	3 teaspoons baking powder
½ cup cream of coconut	1 teaspoon salt

In mixing bowl, cream sugar and butter well. Add eggs, one at a time, blending well after each addition. In another bowl, combine pineapple juice, cream of coconut, coconut extract and rum. Combine flour, baking powder, and salt together. Add pineapple juice mixture to sugar/egg mixture alternately with dry ingredients. Mix well. Pour into two greased and floured 9-inch round cake pans. Bake at 350 degrees for 35 minutes or until top springs back when touched. Cool 15 minutes. Remove from pan and chill on rack. Spread Filling (see recipe below) on layers.

Filling:

½ cup pineapple juice	1½ cups whipping cream
1 tablespoon gelatin	½ cup powdered sugar
1 cup unsweetened crushed pineapple	1 teaspoon coconut extract
	Flaked coconut for garnish

In a small pan, combine pineapple juice and gelatin and let stand 5 minutes. Heat just to dissolve gelatin. Pour into blender and purée with crushed pineapple until smooth. Pour into a bowl and chill until half set. In another bowl, whip cream, powdered sugar, and coconut extract until stiff peaks form. Fold half of whipped cream mixture into chilled pineapple mixture. Spread half of filling on top of one layer. Put other layer on top and spread with remaining filling. Frost sides with reserved whipped cream. Sprinkle with coconut and chill well.

Coconut Pound Cake

1	cup butter	1	teaspoon baking powder
⅔	cup shortening	1	cup milk
3	cups sugar	1	teaspoon coconut extract
5	eggs	1	teaspoon vanilla
3	cups flour	1	cup flaked coconut

In large mixing bowl, cream butter and shortening. Add sugar and beat until light and fluffy. Add eggs, one at a time, beating well after each addition. Combine flour and baking powder together. Add alternately to sugar mixture with milk, beginning and ending with flour mixture. Add flavorings. Stir in coconut. Pour batter into a greased and floured 10-inch fluted bundt pan. Bake at 325 degrees for 1 hour and 30 minutes. Cool for 15 minutes and invert on serving plate.

NOTE: This cake is excellent.

Pineapple Pound Cake

½	cup shortening	1	teaspoon baking powder
1	cup butter	¼	cup milk
2¾	cups sugar	1	teaspoon vanilla
6	eggs	1	cup undrained crushed
3	cups flour		pineapple, in its own juice
½	teaspoon salt	1	cup chopped pecans

In large mixing bowl, cream shortening, butter, and sugar. Add eggs, one at a time, beating well after each addition. Combine flour, salt, and baking powder and add alternately with milk to sugar mixture. Add vanilla. Stir in crushed pineapple and pecans. Blend well. Pour batter into a greased and floured 10-inch bundt pan. Place in cold oven. Bake at 325 degrees for 1 hour and 20 to 30 minutes. Cool in pan 10 minutes, invert and pour Glaze (see recipe below) over cake while hot.

Glaze:

1½	cups powdered sugar	¼	cup butter, softened
1	cup crushed pineapple, drained		

In mixing bowl, combine all ingredients until well blended.

Pineapple Cake

1   (18½-ounce) box butter cake
    mix

Follow directions on package. Bake in three greased and floured 9-inch round cake pans at 325 degrees for 25 minutes. Cool 10 minutes in pan and invert to wire rack to cool completely. Put Filling (see recipe below) in between layers.

Filling:

1   (8-ounce) can crushed pineapple   1   tablespoon cornstarch
    (reserve ¼ cup of juice for   1   tablespoon sugar
    icing)

Combine ingredients in saucepan and cook over low heat, stirring constantly, until thick. Cool slightly and spread between layers. Ice sides and top with Icing (see recipe below).

Icing:

1½ cups sugar   1   teaspoon vanilla
½   cup water   ¼   cup pineapple juice (reserved
½   cup butter, softened   from crushed pineapple)
½   cup flour

Combine sugar and water in saucepan and cook over medium heat. Meanwhile, in mixing bowl, beat butter, flour, and vanilla in small bowl until creamy. Let stand until sugar and water are ready. Test sugar and water by pouring off spoon to form a string (takes approximately 20 to 30 minutes). Then pour slowly over butter mixture, beating constantly. Add half of pineapple juice. When mixture seems creamy, beat at a low speed, adding a little more juice only if needed. This is a thin creamy icing. Pour over cake, beginning at top.

NOTE: This is cake is as moist as it is easy.

Mexican Fruit Cake

1 (20-ounce) can undrained pineapple, in its own juice	2 cups sugar
	1 teaspoon baking soda
2 cups flour	1 cup chopped pecans

Mix all ingredients in large bowl. Pour into a greased and floured 13×9×2-inch baking pan. Bake at 350 degrees for 40 minutes. Frost with Icing (see recipe below).

Icing:

1 (8-ounce) package cream cheese	1 teaspoon vanilla
½ cup butter, softened	2 cups powdered sugar

In large mixing bowl, combine cream cheese and butter until light. Add vanilla and powdered sugar, mixing until well combined. Ice hot cake.

NOTE: There are no eggs in this cake. It is a super cake.

Cajun Cake

2 cups flour	1½ cups sugar
2 eggs	1½ teaspoons baking soda
1 (20-ounce) can crushed pineapple, in its own juice	⅛ teaspoon salt

Mix together all ingredients in bowl and beat by hand 1 minute. Place in a greased and floured 13×9×2-inch baking pan. Bake at 300 degrees for 40 to 45 minutes. Remove from oven and spread with Topping (see recipe below).

Topping:

½ cup butter	1 teaspoon vanilla
1 (5⅓-ounce) can evaporated milk	1 cup chopped pecans
1 cup sugar	1 cup flaked coconut

Mix butter, milk, and sugar in saucepan. Bring mixture to a boil and boil for 5 minutes. Remove from heat and add vanilla, pecans, and coconut. Spread on hot cake. Let cool and cut into squares to serve.

NOTE: Very moist and so good.

Banana Nut Cake with Caramel Icing

3   eggs
1¼ cups sugar
½   cup butter, melted
1   teaspoon vanilla
2½ cups flour
½   teaspoon salt

2½ teaspons baking powder
½   teaspoon baking soda
1¼ cups mashed bananas
2   tablespoons brandy
1¼ cups buttermilk
1   cup chopped pecans

In mixing bowl, beat eggs and sugar until thick. Add butter and vanilla, beating well. In another bowl, combine flour, salt, baking powder, and baking soda. Add flour mixture alternately with combined bananas, brandy, and buttermilk to creamed mixture, beginning and ending with flour mixture. Stir in pecans. Pour batter into two or three greased and floured 9-inch round cake pans. Bake at 350 degrees for 20 to 30 minutes. Cool 15 minutes and remove from pans to cool on racks. Frost cooled cake with Caramel Icing (see recipe below).

Caramel Icing:

¾   cup butter
1½ cups light brown sugar
¼   teaspoon salt
⅓   cup milk
1½ (16-ounce) boxes powdered
      sugar

1   teaspoon vanilla
1   teaspoon brandy (optional)
¾   cup chopped pecans

In heavy saucepan, melt butter. Add brown sugar and salt. Cook over low heat for two minutes, stirring constantly. Add milk and continue stirring until mixture comes to a boil. Remove from heat and beat in powdered sugar. Add vanilla and brandy. Stir in pecans, mixing well.

NOTE: A banana cake is an old favorite. This one is slightly different and assured not to last long.

Carrot Cake

2	cups flour	4	eggs
2	teaspoons baking powder	1½	cups oil
1½	teaspoons baking soda	2	cups finely grated carrots
1	teaspoon salt	1	cup chopped pecans
2	teaspoons cinnamon	1	(8-ounce) can crushed
2	cups sugar		pineapple, drained

Sift together first five ingredients and put in large bowl. Add sugar, eggs, and oil; mixing well. Stir in carrots, pecans, and drained pineapple; blending thoroughly. Pour into three greased and floured 9-inch round cake pans. Bake at 350 degrees for 25 to 30 minutes. Cool briefly in pans, then turn onto racks. Cool completely and ice with Cream Cheese Frosting (see recipe below).

Cream Cheese Frosting:

12	ounces cream cheese	1	teaspoon vanilla
6	tablespoons butter		
1½	(16-ounce) boxes powdered		
	sugar		

In large mixing bowl, beat cream cheese and butter until smooth. Add powdered sugar and beat until light. Add vanilla.

Carrot Walnut Pound Cake

3   cups flour
2   teaspoons baking powder
1   teaspoon baking soda
1   teaspoon cinnamon
½   teaspoon salt
1   cup butter, softened
1   cup light brown sugar
1   cup sugar

4   eggs
2   tablespoons grated lemon rind
2   tablespoons grated orange rind
2   tablespoons lemon juice
2   tablespoons orange juice
1   pound carrots, peeled and grated
1   cup coarsely chopped walnuts

Sift dry ingredients, set aside. In mixing bowl, cream butter, brown sugar, and sugar until light and fluffy. Add eggs, one at a time, beating well after each addition until smooth and light. Combine lemon and orange rinds and juices. Add dry ingredients to sugar mixture alternately with lemon/orange mixture, beginning and ending with dry ingredients. Beat just until smooth. Stir in grated carrots and walnuts, mixing well. Pour batter into greased and floured 10-inch bundt pan. Bake at 350 degrees for 50 minutes. Cool slightly and invert onto serving plate. Top with Cream Cheese Glaze (see recipe below).

Cream Cheese Glaze:

1   (8-ounce) package cream cheese, softened
1   tablespoon lemon juice

1   teaspoon grated lemon rind
1½ cups powdered sugar

In mixing bowl, combine cream cheese, lemon juice, lemon rind, and powdered sugar. Beat until smooth. Spread glaze over top of warm cake, letting it run down side of cake. Can decorate with walnuts.

Upside Down Apple Custard Cake

1½ cups flour
¾ cup sugar
1 tablespoon baking powder
½ teaspoon salt
2 eggs
2 tablespoons milk
1½ tablespoons grated lemon rind
¼ cup butter, melted

½ teaspoon cinnamon
2 cups thinly sliced tart apples, peeled and cored
1 (14-ounce) can sweetened condensed milk
1 cup sour cream
¼ cup lemon juice

Stir flour, ½ cup sugar, baking powder, and salt together. Set aside. In large mixing bowl, beat eggs, milk, and lemon rind. Add the flour mixture gradually and melted butter. Beat on low speed until well blended. Spread evenly in a greased and floured 9 × 9 × 2-inch square pan. Combine remaining ¼ cup sugar and ½ teaspoon cinnamon. Arrange apples on batter and sprinkle with cinnamon-sugar mixture. Bake at 400 degrees for 25 to 30 minutes. Meanwhile, in another bowl combine the condensed milk with sour cream. Stir in the lemon juice. Remove cake from oven and pour cream mixture evenly over the apples. Return to oven and bake 10 minutes longer or until just bubbly. Serve warm or chilled. Refrigerate leftovers. Yield: 8 to 10 servings.

NOTE: This is an unusual cake that is not too sweet.

Apple Cake with Broiled Topping

3 eggs
1½ cups shortening
2 cups sugar
2 cups flour
1 teaspoon baking soda
1 teaspoon cinnamon
1 teaspoon baking powder
⅛ teaspoon salt
4 cups chopped tart apples, peeled and cored
1 cup chopped pecans

In large mixing bowl, cream eggs, shortening, and sugar. Sift dry ingredients together and blend into creamed mixture. Fold in apples and pecans. Pour batter into a greased and floured 13×9×2-inch baking pan. Bake at 350 degrees for 40 to 50 minutes. About 10 minutes before cake is done, prepare Topping (see recipe below).

Topping:

½ cup butter
¼ cup evaporated milk
¾ cup light brown sugar
1 teaspoon vanilla
1 cup flaked coconut
1 cup chopped pecans

Mix butter, evaporated milk, sugar, and vanilla in saucepan and bring to a boil. Add coconut and pecans. When cake is done, spread hot Topping over hot cake and broil until slightly brown. (Watch carefully).

Strawberry Crumb Cake

2 cups flour	¾ cup milk
4 teaspoons baking powder	½ teaspoon lemon extract
½ cup sugar	1 teaspoon vanilla
½ teaspoon salt	

In mixing bowl, combine all ingredients and mix well (mixture will be quite thick). Spread in a greased 10-inch springform or 9×9×2-inch square baking pan. Sprinkle with Sugared Strawberries (see recipe below).

Sugared Strawberries:

2 cups fresh strawberries	½ cup sugar

Slice and stem strawberries. Sprinkle strawberries and sugar on top of cake. Top with Topping (see recipe below).

Topping:

⅓ cup sugar	⅓ cup butter, softened
⅓ cup flour	¼ teaspoon nutmeg

In another bowl, mix all ingredients with a fork until crumbly. Sprinkle over strawberries, then bake at 425 degrees for 30 to 40 minutes. Serve warm with whipped cream. Yield: 10 to 12 servings.

NOTE: Any fresh fruit can be substituted.

Butterscotch Cake

⅔ cup butterscotch chips
½ cup butter
2 cups sugar
3 eggs
2 cups flour

1 teaspoon salt
1 teaspoon baking powder
1 teaspoon baking soda
1 cup buttermilk

Melt the chips in microwave or in top of double boiler. In mixing bowl, cream the butter and add the sugar gradually. Add one egg at a time, beating well after each addition. Sift dry ingredients together. Mix in the melted chips and the dry ingredients, alternating with the buttermilk. Pour batter into three greased and floured 8-inch round cake pans. Bake at 375 degrees for 20 to 25 minutes. Cool in pans and then invert on cooling racks. Spread Filling (see recipe below) between layers and on top of cake.

Filling:

½ cup sugar
½ cup evaporated milk
1 tablespoon cornstarch
⅓ cup water
⅓ cup butterscotch chips

1 egg yolk
2 tablespoons butter
1 cup flaked coconut
1 cup chopped pecans

Combine the sugar, milk, cornstarch, water, butterscotch chips, and egg yolk in saucepan. Cook over low heat, stirring until thick enough to spread. Remove from heat and add butter, coconut, and pecans. Spread between the layers and on top of the cake. Cover sides of cake with Cream Cheese Icing (see recipe below).

Cream Cheese Icing:

4 ounces cream cheese
2 tablespoons butter

1 (16-ounce) box powdered sugar
1 tablespoon evaporated milk

Mix the above ingredients in mixing bowl and ice the sides of the cake.

NOTE: This reminds you of a butterscotch German Chocolate Cake. Rich, moist, and delicious.

Pecan Praline Cake

½ cup butter	2 cups flour
1 cup buttermilk	1 teaspoon baking soda
2 cups light brown sugar	1 teaspoon vanilla
2 eggs	

In small saucepan or microwave, heat together butter and buttermilk until warm. Put mixture in bowl and add sugar and eggs, beating well. Sift dry ingredients. Add to creamed mixture, mixing well. Add vanilla. (Batter will be thin). Pour into a greased and floured 13×9×2-inch baking pan and bake at 325 degrees for 25 minutes. Remove from oven and spread with Topping (see recipe below).

Topping:

½ cup butter, softened	⅓ cup evaporated milk
1 cup light brown sugar	1 cup chopped pecans

Combine all ingredients except pecans and beat well with a mixer. Add pecans. Spread on cake and return to oven and broil until the topping bubbles and is slightly browned. Cool before serving and cut into squares.

NOTE: A fantastic cake.

White Chocolate Pound Cake

2 tablespoons white vinegar	1 teaspoon butter flavoring
1 cup evaporated milk	½ teaspoon salt
2¼ cups flour	4 eggs
2 cups sugar	4 ounces white chocolate, melted
¾ cup shortening	and cooled
1 teaspoon baking soda	1 cup flaked coconut
1 teaspoon vanilla	1 cup chopped pecans

Stir vinegar into milk; let stand until slightly thickened, about 1 minute. In mixing bowl, beat vinegar mixture and remaining ingredients except coconut and pecans on low speed until blended. Then beat on high speed, scraping bowl occasionally, 3 minutes. Stir in coconut and pecans. Pour into a greased and floured 10-inch bundt pan. Bake at 350 degrees for 50 to 55 minutes, or until toothpick inserted in center comes out clean. Do not overcook. Cool 15 minutes. Invert on wire rack or heatproof serving plate.

NOTE: This is so good you cannot stop eating it.

Old Fashioned Chocolate Cake

1   cup butter
2   cups sugar
4   eggs
2   cups flour
¼   teaspoon salt
1½ teaspoons baking soda

⅔   cup buttermilk
1   teaspoon vanilla
3   (1-ounce) squares unsweetened
     chocolate, melted in ⅔ cup
     boiling water

In large mixing bowl, cream butter and sugar until light and fluffy. Add eggs, one at a time, beating well after each addition. Sift flour with salt. Mix baking soda with buttermilk and add alternately with flour to creamed mixture, starting and ending with flour. Add vanilla and melted chocolate with water; stir until smooth. Pour batter into a greased and floured 13×9×2-inch baking pan and bake at 325 degrees for 45 minutes. While slightly warm, ice with Chocolate Frosting (see recipe below).

Chocolate Frosting:

½   cup butter
1½ cups sugar
⅓   cup milk

¾   cup semi-sweet chocolate chips
1   cup chopped pecans
1   teaspoon vanilla

In a heavy saucepan, cook butter, sugar, and milk until boils. Boil for 2 minutes. Remove from heat; add chocolate chips and pecans. Blend quickly. Beat until spreading consistency. (It won't take more than a minute or two). Spread at once over chocolate cake.

NOTE: A light chocolate cake with a rich frosting. It's too good to pass by.

Chocolate Pecan Cake

1 cup butter	1 cup flour
1 cup sugar	1 teaspoon vanilla
4 eggs	1 cup chopped pecans
1 (16-ounce) can chocolate syrup	

In mixing bowl, cream butter and sugar until light and fluffy. Add eggs, one at a time, beating well after each addition. Add chocolate syrup and flour alternately to creamed mixture. Add vanilla. Stir in pecans. Pour batter into a greased and floured 13×9×2-inch baking pan. Bake at 350 degrees for 25 to 30 minutes. Frost cooled cake with Chocolate Frosting (see recipe below).

Chocolate Frosting:

½ cup butter	⅓ cup milk
1 cup sugar	1 teaspoon vanilla
¼ cup cocoa	1 cup chopped pecans

Combine all ingredients except vanilla and pecans in heavy saucepan over low heat. Bring to a boil and boil for one minute. Remove from heat and add vanilla and pecans. Beat to desired consistency. Spread on cooled cake.

Chocolate Oatmeal Cake

1½ cups boiling water	2 eggs
1 cup old fashioned oatmeal	1 teaspoon vanilla
½ cup butter	1½ cups flour
½ (4-ounce) bar German-sweet chocolate	1 teaspoon baking soda
	½ teaspoon salt
1 cup sugar	1 cup semi-sweet chocolate chips
1 cup light brown sugar	1 cup chopped pecans

Pour 1½ cups boiling water over oatmeal. Add butter and German chocolate. Let stand 20 minutes. Stir to combine and make sure butter and chocolate are melted. Add sugar, brown sugar, eggs, vanilla, flour, baking soda, and salt to oatmeal mixture. Stir well. Pour batter into a greased and floured 13×9×2-inch baking pan. Sprinkle with chocolate chips and pecans. Bake at 350 degrees for 35 minutes.

NOTE: This is super quick to make, moist, and not too rich.

Chocolate Zucchini Cake

2½ cups flour
1   teaspoon baking powder
1   teaspoon baking soda
4   tablespoons cocoa
1   teaspoon cinnamon
½   cup shortening
½   cup butter, softened
1   cup sugar

3   eggs
½   cup buttermilk
2   teaspoons vanilla
3   cups finely shredded unpeeled
    zucchini
½   cup semi-sweet chocolate chips
2   tablespoons sugar

In mixing bowl, combine dry ingredients. In large mixing bowl, cream shortening and butter with 1 cup sugar until light and fluffy. Add eggs, one at a time, beating after each addition. Alternately add dry ingredients, buttermilk, and zucchini, mixing well. Add vanilla. Pour half of the batter into a greased and floured 10-inch bundt pan. Sprinkle with chocolate chips which have been mixed with the 2 tablespoons of sugar. Cover with remaining batter and bake at 325 degrees for 50 minutes. Allow to cool for 10 minutes and invert onto serving platter.

NOTE: No one will ever guess the ingredients of this moist, chocolately cake.

Chocolate Cake with Coconut Topping

½   cup cocoa
½   cup boiling water
½   cup butter
1½ cups sugar
2   eggs
½   cup buttermilk

1   teaspoon baking soda
2   cups flour
¼   teaspoon salt
1   tablespoon vanilla
1   (18-ounce) can grated coconut
    in heavy syrup

Mix cocoa with boiling water in small bowl. Set aside. In large mixing bowl, cream butter and sugar until light and fluffy. Add eggs, mixing well. Blend in cocoa mixture. To buttermilk, add baking soda and blend into chocolate mixture. Combine flour and salt and add to chocolate mixture. Add vanilla. Pour batter into a greased and floured 13×9×2-inch baking pan and bake at 350 degrees for 20 to 25 minutes. Remove from oven and poke holes with toothpick along top of cake. Spread on hot cake the can of grated coconut in heavy syrup.

Double Chocolate Cake

½ cup butter
2 (1-ounce) squares unsweetened
   chocolate
½ cup oil
¼ cup water
½ cup buttermilk

2 cups flour
2 cups sugar
2 eggs, beaten
1 teaspoon baking soda
1 teaspoon vanilla

Melt butter and chocolate in microwave or in top of double boiler. Pour into a large bowl. Add oil and water, mixing well. Stirring with wooden spoon, add remaining ingredients, mixing thoroughly. Pour batter into three greased and floured 9-inch round cake pans. Bake at 350 degrees for 20 to 25 minutes. Cool 10 minutes in pan and invert to cooling racks. Spread Chocolate Cream Cheese Icing (see recipe below) between layers and frost top and sides with Chocolate Pudding Icing (see recipe below).

Chocolate Cream Cheese Icing:

1 (3-ounce) package cream cheese
2 tablespoons butter
1 tablespoon cocoa

1½ cups powdered sugar
½ teaspoon vanilla
½ cup chopped pecans

In mixing bowl, blend cream cheese and butter until light. Add cocoa, powdered sugar, and vanilla, mixing well. Add pecans. Spread between layers.

Chocolate Pudding Icing:

3 (1-ounce) squares unsweetened
   chocolate
1½ cups sugar
1¾ cups boiling water
½ cup cold water

¼ teaspoon salt
4 heaping tablespoons cornstarch
4 tablespoons butter
2 teaspoons vanilla

In top of double boiler or in heavy saucepan, melt chocolate. Remove from heat and add sugar, stirring until well mixed. Pour boiling water over chocolate mixture, stir, and set aside. Make a paste out of the cold water, salt, and cornstarch. Pour paste into chocolate mixture, stirring well. Return mixture to heat and bring to a boil, cooking and stirring until pudding thickens. Remove from heat and add butter and vanilla. Return to heat, cover and cook for 10 minutes on very low heat. Do not uncover. Let pudding cool, beating occasionally. Spread cooled pudding on sides and top of cake.

NOTE: This is an irresistible chocolate cake. The Pudding Icing is great and can be used on any chocolate cake.

Unusual Chocolate Layer Cake

2	cups flour	1	cup water
1	teaspoon baking soda	2	cups sugar
½	cup butter	2	eggs
½	cup oil	½	cup buttermilk
3	(1-ounce) squares unsweetened chocolate	1	teaspoon vanilla

Sift flour and baking soda; set aside. In small saucepan, heat butter, oil, and chocolate over low heat until chocolate is melted. Add 1 cup water. Cool. To flour mixture, add sugar, eggs, buttermilk, and vanilla. Combine with wooden spoon. Stir in cooled chocolate mixture just to combine. Pour batter into two greased and floured 9-inch round cake pans. Bake at 350 degrees for 25 to 30 mintues, or until cake springs back to touch. Cool 5 minutes and turn out on racks. Cool. Spread Filling (see recipe below) between layers.

Filling:

1	(5⅓-ounce) can evaporated milk	1	teaspoon vanilla
¾	cup sugar	½	cup chopped pecans
¼	cup raisins	½	cup whipping cream, whipped
½	cup chopped dates		

Combine all ingredients except vanilla, pecans, and cream and cook over medium heat until thickened, approximately 5 minutes. Add vanilla and pecans. Cool. Spread cooled Filling on bottom layer and then whipped cream. Top with second layer and cover cake with Frosting (see recipe below).

Frosting:

1	(6-ounce) package semi-sweet chocolate chips	½	cup sour cream
			Dash salt

In top of double boiler or microwave, melt chocolate. Stir in sour cream and salt. Beat with wooden spoon until smooth. Cool 5 minutes and spread over cake.

NOTE: A fabulous chocolate cake that is a little different.

Chocolate Torte

Torte:

5½ (1-ounce) squares semi-sweet
  chocolate
¾ cup butter, softened
¾ cup sugar
2 tablespoons flour
1½ cups chopped pecans

6 eggs, separated
2 tablespoons instant coffee,
  dissolved in as little water as
  possible (optional)
⅓ cup currant jelly

Melt chocolate in top of double boiler or microwave and cool slightly. In mixing bowl, cream butter and sugar until light and fluffy. Combine flour and pecans. Set aside. Add egg yolks to creamed mixture, one at a time, beating well after each addition. Add melted chocolate and coffee, mixing well. Add flour and pecans. In another bowl, beat egg whites until stiff. Fold in beaten egg whites into chocolate batter. Grease and flour two 9-inch round cake pans and then place a wax paper circle over entire bottom, greasing and flouring again. Pour batter into prepared pans. Bake at 350 degrees for 20 to 25 minutes. Cool and invert on cooling rack. Place bottom layer on serving plate and spread top with currant jelly. Next, cover with Filling (see recipe below).

Filling:

1 (4-serving) box instant
  chocolate fudge pudding
⅛ cup very strong coffee

4 (1 3/16-ounce) English toffee
  candy bars, crushed

Prepare pudding according to directions on package, using only 1½ cups cold milk and coffee. Spoon pudding over currant jelly, using only enough so top layer will not push it out the sides. Sprinkle crushed candy bars over pudding. Top with other cake layer and ice sides and top with Whipped Cream Topping (see recipe below).

Whipped Cream Topping:

2 cups whipping cream
2 tablespoons powdered sugar
1 teaspoon vanilla

4 (1 3/16-ounce) English toffee
  candy bars, crushed

In mixing bowl, beat whipping cream until soft peaks form. Add powdered sugar and vanilla. Frost sides and top of cake. Sprinkle with crushed candy bars.

NOTE: Everyone will want this recipe when you serve this spectacular chocolate torte.

Red Velvet Cake

1 (1-ounce) bottle red food coloring	2½ cups cake flour
4½ tablespoons cocoa	½ teaspoon salt
¾ cup butter	1½ teaspoons baking soda
2¼ cups sugar	1½ teaspoons vanilla
3 eggs	1 teaspoon butter flavoring
1½ cups buttermilk	1½ teaspoons vinegar

In small bowl, mix red food coloring and cocoa with fork; set aside. In mixing bowl, cream butter and sugar until light and fluffy. Add eggs, mixing well. Add cocoa mixture to butter mixture and beat well. Sift flour with salt and baking soda and add alternately with buttermilk to creamed mixture, beginning and ending with flour. Mix well. Fold in vanilla, butter flavoring, and vinegar. Pour into two greased and floured 9-inch round cake pans. Bake at 350 degrees for 30 to 35 minutes. Cool layers on racks. Frost cake with Special Frosting (see recipe below) after cools completely.

Special Frosting:

3 tablespoons flour	1 cup butter
1 cup milk	1 teaspoon vanilla
1 cup sugar	Chopped nuts (optional)

In small saucepan, cook flour and milk over low heat until very thick, stirring constantly. *Cool* completely. In large mixing bowl, cream sugar, butter, and vanilla until fluffy. Add cooled flour mixture; beat well. Spread between layers and on top and sides of cake.

Doberge Cake

½ cup butter	3 cups cake flour
½ cup shortening	3 teaspoons baking powder
2 cups sugar	½ cup milk
¼ teaspoon salt	½ cup water
4 eggs, separated	1 teaspoon vanilla

In mixing bowl, cream butter, shortening, sugar, and salt together until light and fluffy. Add egg yolks and blend until smooth. Sift together flour and baking powder and add alternately with combined milk and water to the creamed mixture. Beat until blended. Add vanilla. In another bowl, beat egg whites until stiff. Fold into batter. Grease 9-inch round cake pans and line with waxed paper and grease and flour again. Pour ¾ cup batter into each pan, spreading evenly over bottom of pan. Bake at 375 degrees for 12 to 15 minutes or until very lightly browned. Remove cake to cake rack and repeat baking process until batter is entirely used. The result is 8 thin (¼-½ inch) layers. When cool, put layers together with chilled Chocolate Cream Filling (see recipe below), reserving top layer for frosting. Chill before frosting top layer and sides of doberge with thin Chocolate Frosting (see recipe next page). Doberge may be refrigerated for several days.

Chocolate Cream Filling:

2 cups sugar	2 whole eggs and 4 yolks, slightly
10 tablespoons cornstarch	beaten
2 teaspoons salt	2 teaspoons vanilla
4 cups milk	
4 (1-ounce) squares unsweetened chocolate, cut up	

Mix together sugar, cornstarch, salt, milk, and chocolate in 1½-quart saucepan. Bring to boil over medium heat, stirring constantly. Boil 1½ minutes. Remove from heat and pour a small amount of mixture over slightly beaten eggs and yolks. Blend into hot mixture and cook over very low heat, stirring until thick, for about 2 minutes. Remove from heat and add vanilla. Chill until filling sets.

Continued on next page

Chocolate Frosting:

½ cup butter
8 (1-ounce) squares semi-sweet
   chocolate

1 (16-ounce) box powdered sugar
½ cup boiling water

In saucepan, melt together butter and chocolate over very low heat. Remove from heat. Blend in sugar and water and beat until smooth. Frost top and sides of doberge.

NOTE: This impressive cake is a favorite in New Orleans.

Tunnel of Fudge Cake

1½ cups butter
6 eggs
1½ cups sugar
1 teaspoon vanilla

2 cups flour
1 (13.7-ounce) package fudge
   frosting mix
2 cups chopped walnuts

In large mixing bowl, cream butter until fluffy. Add eggs, one at a time, beating well after each addition. Gradually add sugar; continue beating until light and fluffy. Add vanilla. By hand, stir in flour, frosting mix, and walnuts until well blended. Pour batter into a greased and floured 10-inch bundt pan. Bake at 350 degrees for 50 to 60 minutes. Cake is done when top is dry and shiny. Cool 2 hours in pan and then remove.

NOTE: There will be a "tunnel of fudge" in the middle of cake.

Incredible Chocolate Cake

½ cup butter	½ teaspoon salt
2 cups sugar	2 teaspoons baking powder
2 eggs	1½ cups milk
3 (1-ounce) squares unsweetened	2 teaspoons vanilla
chocolate, melted	1 cup chopped pecans
2 cups flour	

In mixing bowl, cream butter and sugar until light and fluffy. Add eggs, mixing well. Blend in melted chocolate. Combine flour, salt, and baking powder together. Add to creamed mixture alternately with milk, beginning and ending with dry ingredients. Add vanilla and pecans. Pour batter into three greased and floured 9-inch round cake pans. Bake at 350 degrees for 30 minutes. Cool in pan 10 minutes and invert onto cooling racks. Cool completely and carefully split each layer in half to make 6 thin layers. (Only split layers as ready to use because they will break easily—if do break, piece back together). Spread Chocolate Frosting (see recipe below) between layers and on top and sides of cake. Refrigerate.

Chocolate Frosting:

1½ cups butter	1 tablespoon lemon juice
2 (1-ounce) squares unsweetened	2 eggs, beaten
chocolate	1 teaspoon vanilla
1½ (16-ounce) boxes powdered	2 cups chopped pecans
sugar	

In microwave or in heavy saucepan, melt butter and chocolate. Remove from heat and add remaining ingredients, mixing by hand, until well combined. Carefully frost cake.

Chocolate Mousse Cake

1 (12-ounce) package semi-sweet chocolate chips	1½ tablespoons coffee cream liqueur
½ cup butter	1 teaspoon vanilla
6 eggs, separated, room temperature	Pinch cream of tartar
1 cup sugar	2 cups whipping cream
¾ cup chopped pecans	¼ cup powdered sugar
	1 tablespoon coffee cream liqueur

Melt chocolate chips and butter in top of double boiler or microwave. Beat egg yolks with mixer in large bowl until very thick, about 5 minutes. Beat in ½ cup sugar, 1 tablespoon at a time. Stir in melted chocolate, pecans, 1½ tablespoons liqueur, and vanilla. In large bowl, beat egg whites with cream of tartar until soft peaks form. Gradually add remaining ½ cup sugar and beat until stiff, but not dry. Gently fold ¼ of whites into chocolate mixture, then fold chocolate mixture back into remaining whites. Pour into greased and floured 10-inch springform pan. Bake at 350 degrees for 30 minutes. Reduce oven temperature to 275 degrees and continue baking another 30 minutes. Turn off oven, let cake stand in oven for 30 minutes with door ajar. Remove cake from oven. Dampen paper towel and place on top of cake for 5 minutes, remove towel (top of cake will crack and fall). Cool cake in pan. Remove springform. In large bowl, beat whipping cream until soft peaks form. Beat in powdered sugar and 1 tablespoon liqueur. Spoon whipped cream onto top of cake. Refrigerate 6 hours.

NOTE: This cake will always be a favorite—a nice combination.

Black Forest Cake

1	(18½-ounce) box devil's food cake mix	1	(16-ounce) can pitted dark sweet cherries
1	cup sour cream	2	tablespoons sugar
1	(4-serving) package instant chocolate fudge pudding	1	tablespoon cornstarch
1	cup milk	1	cup whipping cream
½	teaspoon vanilla	½	cup sliced almonds, toasted

Prepare cake mix according to directions on package and bake in a greased and floured 13 × 9 × 2-inch baking pan for 25 to 30 minutes. Do not overbake. Cool completely. In mixing bowl, beat sour cream, instant pudding, ½cup milk and vanilla until mixture is fluffy. Gradually add remaining milk, beating until smooth. Spread over cooled chocolate cake. Refrigerate. Drain cherries, reserving ¾ cup of syrup. In saucepan, combine sugar and cornstarch. Gradually stir in reserved syrup. Cook and stir over medium heat until thick and bubbly. Add drained cherries and cool. Spread over chilled pudding. Cover and chill overnight. Before serving, whip cream until stiff peaks form and spread over cherries. Sprinkle with almonds. Refrigerate.

NOTE: This is an easy version to this great cake.

Chocolate Chip Cream Cheese Cake

1½ cups butter, softened
12 ounces cream cheese
3 cups sugar
6 eggs
3 cups flour

½ teaspoon salt
1 tablespoon vanilla
1 (12-ounce) package semi-sweet
   chocolate chips

In a large mixing bowl, cream butter and cream cheese until well combined. Blend in sugar, 1 cup at a time, mixing well. Add eggs, one at a time, beating well after each addition. Combine flour and salt. Add flour mixture gradually, blending until smooth. Add vanilla. Stir in chocolate chips. Pour batter into a greased and floured 10-inch bundt pan. Bake at 325 degrees for 1 hour and 15 minutes or until done. Check cake after 1 hour. Cool in pan 20 minutes, then invert on serving dish.

NOTE: This pound cake is unbelievable — it is so moist and full of chocolate. It is one you will want to have in your home for any occasion.

Pies

Cream Cheese Pastry

1 cup flour	1 (3-ounce) package cream cheese
½ cup butter	

Combine flour and butter in bowl. Using fingertips, rub your fingers through the dough until mixture resembles coarse meal. Add cream cheese and continue to rub until dough is smooth. Press dough into a 9-inch pie plate. Bake as directed in recipe.

NOTE: For those who are scared of rolling pie crusts, this is the one for you. It has a wonderful flavor, as well as it is easy.

Pie Crust

1 cup flour	⅓ cup shortening
½ teaspoon salt	2½ tablespoons cold water

Combine flour and salt in small bowl. Cut in shortening with fork until mixture resembles coarse crumbs. Mix in water, stirring until mixture will form into a ball. Roll dough out on floured surface about 2 inches larger than inverted pie plate. Use overhanging edge of pastry to form a rim around pie. Crust can be used in any recipe calling for an unbaked crust. If the recipe calls for a baked pie shell, prick bottom and sides thoroughly with fork and bake at 475 degrees for 8 to 10 minutes before filling.

Apple Crumble Pie

1	9-inch unbaked cream cheese pie shell (See Page 98)	¼	cup light brown sugar
		1	tablespoon flour
5	to 6 cups peeled, cored and thinly sliced tart apples	1	teaspoon cinnamon
		2	tablespoons cold water
¾	cup sugar	1	tablespoon butter, melted

In unbaked pie shell, arrange apple slices. Combine sugars, flour, and cinnamon together in a small bowl. Add water and butter. Toss with apples and distribute evenly in pie shell. Crumble Topping (see recipe below) on top of apple mixture. Bake at 425 degrees for 10 minutes. Reduce oven to 325 degrees and continue baking for 1 hour. Remove pie from oven and cool slightly. Drizzle Glaze (see recipe below) over warm pie.

Topping:

¼	cup sugar	1	cup flour
¼	cup light brown sugar	½	cup butter, softened
½	teaspoon cinnamon		

In small bowl, combine sugars, cinnamon, and flour. Cut in butter with pastry blender or fork until mixture is crumbly. Crumble over apple mixture in shell and bake as directed.

Glaze:

½	cup powdered sugar	2	tablespoons lemon juice

In small bowl, mix together sugar and lemon juice with fork until smooth. Drizzle over warm pie.

NOTE: One of the best apple pies you will ever have. Serve warm with ice cream and you will definitely be a hit.

Classic Banana Cream Pie

Pastry Shell:

1½ cups flour	1 tablespoon oil
¼ cup butter, cubed	1 tablespoon sugar
1 egg yolk	Cold water

In mixing bowl, blend flour and butter until mixture resembles coarse meal. Combine egg yolk, oil, and sugar; adding cold water to make ⅓ cup liquid. Stir into dry mixture until just combined. Shape into ball. Cover with plastic wrap and refrigerate 30 minutes. Roll to fit into a 9-inch pie plate. Prick with fork and bake at 375 degrees for 15 minutes, or until golden. Cool. Fill with Pastry Cream (see recipe below).

Pastry Cream:

2 egg yolks	1 tablespoon vanilla
½ cup sugar	3 firm, medium bananas, peeled
¼ cup flour	and sliced
2 cups milk, scalded	1 cup whipping cream
¼ cup unsalted butter	2 tablespoons sugar

In heavy saucepan, beat egg yolks, ½ cup sugar, and flour until pale lemon color. Beat hot milk into egg mixture. Cook, stirring constantly, until sauce thickens, about 5 minutes. Remove from heat. Stir in butter and vanilla until blended. Transfer to a bowl and cover well by putting plastic wrap directly on top of sauce. Chill in refrigerator. Fold in bananas, reserving a few slices for garnish, if desired. Spoon into pastry shell. Whip cream with 2 tablespoons sugar until stiff peaks form. Spread on pie. Refrigerate.

NOTE: The homemade custard with bananas makes this pie terrific.

Fresh Blueberry Cream Pie

1 cup sour cream	2½ cups fresh blueberries
2 tablespoons flour	1 9-inch unbaked pie shell
¾ cup sugar	3 tablespoons flour
1 teaspoon vanilla	3 tablespoons butter, softened
¼ teaspoon salt	3 tablespoons chopped pecans or
1 egg, beaten	walnuts

In a mixing bowl, combine sour cream, 2 tablespoons flour, sugar, vanilla, salt, and egg, beating well or until smooth. Fold in blueberries. Pour filling into unbaked pie shell. Bake at 400 degrees for 25 minutes. In a small bowl, combine 3 tablespoons flour, butter, and chopped nuts, stirring well. Sprinkle over top of pie. Bake for 10 minutes more. Chill before serving. Yield: 8 servings.

NOTE: Absolutely delicious.

Strawberry Pie

9 ounces lemon-lime soft drink	1 (3-ounce) package cream cheese,
1 cup sugar	softened
4 tablespoons cornstarch	1 cup whipping cream, whipped
¼ teaspoon red food coloring	1 9-inch baked pie shell
1 pint fresh strawberries	

In heavy saucepan, combine lemon-lime soft drink, sugar, and cornstarch and cook over low heat until thick. Add red food coloring. Put in refrigerator to cool. Wash, drain, core and slice strawberries. Set aside. Spread softened cream cheese on bottom of cooled baked pie shell. Lay berries on top of cream cheese layer. Pour chilled sauce on top of berries. Cover strawberry pie with whipped cream. Refrigerate.

NOTE: When strawberry season comes around, this pie will be a favorite.

Key Lime Pie

Crust:

1¼ cups graham cracker crumbs
¼ cup butter, melted

¼ cup light brown sugar
1 teaspoon cinnamon

Combine all ingredients in bowl, mixing well. Press crumb mixture into a 9-inch pie plate. Bake at 350 degrees for 10 minutes. Cool and fill with Key Lime Filling (see recipe below).

Key Lime Filling:

4 egg yolks
1 (14-ounce) can sweetened
condensed milk
½ cup Key lime juice

Grated rind of lime
¼ teaspoon cream of tartar
4 egg whites, separated
½ cup sugar

In mixing bowl, beat yolks until thick and lemon-colored. Add milk and blend. Add juice, 2 tablespoons at a time, beating well after each addition. Add grated lime rind. In another bowl, beat 1 egg white until stiff. Fold egg white into milk-juice mixture. Pour into prepared crust. In same bowl, beat remaining 3 egg whites with cream of tartar until frothy. Gradually beat in sugar, 2 tablespoons at a time, beating after each addition. Beat at high speed until stiff peaks form. Spread carefully over Lime Filling, sealing to edge of the crust and swirling top decoratively. Bake at 400 degrees for 7 to 9 minutes or until meringue is golden. Let pie cool to room temperature and then refrigerate until completely chilled.

NOTE: Can substitute limes if Key limes are not available.

Lemon Ice Box Pie

1	cup graham cracker crumbs	1	cup evaporated milk
2	tablespoons sugar	3	egg yolks, beaten
¼	cup butter, melted	4	tablespoons lemon juice
1	cup sugar	1	teaspoon grated lemon rind
3	tablespoons cornstarch	1	teaspoon vanilla
1	cup milk		

Combine crumbs, 2 tablespoons sugar and melted butter together in a small bowl. Spread into a 9-inch pie plate. Bake at 325 degrees for 10 minutes. Combine 1 cup sugar and cornstarch in medium saucepan. Add milks and cook over medium heat until thick, stirring constantly. Combine egg yolks, lemon juice, and lemon rind together. Add a little of hot milk mixture to egg mixture and then pour all back into saucepan and continue cooking until thick. Add vanilla. Remove from heat. Pour into pie shell and cool completely. Top with whipped cream, if desired.

Mystery Pie

20	finely crushed buttery round crackers	¼	teaspoon cream of tartar
1	cup finely chopped pecans or finely chopped peanuts	1	teaspoon vanilla
		1	(8-ounce) container whipped topping
1	cup sugar, divided	1	(1-ounce) square unsweetened chocolate
3	egg whites		

In large bowl, combine crushed crackers, nuts, and ½ cup sugar, mixing well. In mixing bowl, beat egg whites until frothy. Add cream of tartar and vanilla and continue beating, gradually adding remaining ½ cup sugar, until stiff peaks form. Fold egg whites into cracker mixture, blending until all ingredients are moist. Pour into an ungreased 9-inch pie plate. Bake at 350 degrees for 20 to 30 minutes. Pie will have crusty appearance. Let cool completely. Top with whipped topping and grate chocolate over top of pie. Refrigerate 3 to 4 hours before serving.

NOTE: A real winner.

Famous Pecan Pie

¾ cup butter
1 cup sugar
¼ teaspoon salt
2 eggs, beaten

1 cup light corn syrup
1 teaspoon vanilla
1½ cups chopped pecans
1 9-inch unbaked pie shell

In mixing bowl, cream butter and sugar until light. Add salt. Mix in beaten eggs, corn syrup, vanilla, and pecans, mixing well. Pour batter into pie shell. Bake at 300 degrees for 1 hour or until done.

Black Bottom Pecan Pie

Fudge Filling:

3 tablespoons butter, melted
⅓ cup cocoa
2 eggs
¾ cup sugar

½ teaspoon vanilla
¼ teaspoon salt
1 9-inch unbaked pie shell

In mixing bowl, combine butter and cocoa. Add remaining ingredients, blending well. Pour into pastry lined pan. Bake at 350 degrees for 20 minutes. Remove from oven and top with Pecan Topping (see recipe below).

Pecan Topping:

½ cup light corn syrup
¼ cup sugar
1 tablespoon butter, melted

1 teaspoon vanilla
2 eggs
1 cup pecan halves

In mixing bowl, combine all ingredients, blending well. Add pecans. Pour over partially baked filling. Return to oven and continue baking 30 to 35 minutes or until crust is light golden brown.

NOTE: This pie will attract both pecan pie and chocolate lovers.

Pecan Custard Pie

¼ cup butter, melted	1 cup light corn syrup
¾ cup sugar	1 (5⅓-ounce) can evaporated milk
1 teaspoon vanilla	1 teaspoon vanilla
2 tablespoons flour	1½ cups chopped pecans
½ teaspoon salt	1 9-inch unbaked pie shell
3 eggs	

In small bowl, combine butter, sugar, vanilla, flour, and salt. Mix well. Add eggs, one at a time, beating well after each addition. Blend in syrup, milk, vanilla, and pecans. Mix well. Pour into unbaked pie shell. Bake 10 minutes at 450 degrees; reduce oven temperature to 325 degrees and bake 50 minutes longer or until firm.

NOTE: Absolutely delicious.

Maple Pecan Pumpkin Pie

1 (16-ounce) can solid packed pumpkin	½ teaspoon cinnamon
	½ teaspoon salt
1 (14-ounce) can sweetened condensed milk	¼ teaspoon ginger
	1 teaspoon nutmeg
2 eggs	1 9-inch unbaked pie shell
1 teaspoon maple flavoring	

In large bowl, combine all ingredients. Mix well and pour into pie shell. Bake at 425 degrees for 15 minutes. Then reduce oven temperature to 350 degrees and continue baking 25 minutes. Remove from oven. Spoon Pecan Topping (see recipe below) evenly over top. Return to oven and bake 15 to 20 minutes longer or until golden brown. Cool. Refrigerate leftovers.

Pecan Topping:

1 egg	1 tablespoon butter, melted
3 tablespoons dark corn syrup	½ teaspoon maple flavoring
3 tablespoons light brown sugar	1 cup chopped pecans

In small mixing bowl, beat egg and add corn syrup, brown sugar, butter, and maple flavoring, beating well. Stir in pecans.

NOTE: This is great for the holiday season.

Macadamia-Chocolate Chip Pie

Dough:

2 cups flour	¾ cup chilled shortening
½ teaspoon salt	5 to 7 tablespoons cold orange juice

In bowl, mix flour and salt together. Cut in shortening with a pastry blender until mixture resembles coarse crumbs. Add orange juice until mixture holds together. Dough can be made in a food processor. Chill dough in refrigerator. Roll dough out on a floured surface and press firmly into a greased tart pan or large pie plate. Refrigerate prepared tart shell while making filling. Fill with Filling (see recipe below).

Filling:

¾ cup light brown sugar	1 tablespoon vanilla
¾ teaspoon salt	3 ounces butter, melted
2¼ tablespoons flour	2 cups chopped macademia nuts
1½ cups dark corn syrup	1 (6-ounce) package semi-sweet
5 eggs	chocolate chips

In mixing bowl, combine brown sugar, salt, and flour. Add dark corn syrup and eggs, mixing thoroughly. Add vanilla and melted butter. Mix well. Place nuts and chocolate chips on bottom of chilled tart shell. Add filling almost to the top of the shell. Bake at 275 degrees for 40 to 50 minutes. When pie is done, filling will be set and crust golden. Cool and top with Whipped Cream Topping (see recipe below).

Whipped Cream Topping:

2 cups whipping cream	1 tablespoon premium bourbon, if
Dash of vanilla	desired
2 tablespoons sugar	

Place cream in chilled bowl and whip until whipped cream consistency is reached. Add the remaining ingredients. Top cool pie.

NOTE: Macadamia nuts and chocolate make this pie one that you will not want to miss!

Peanut Butter Pie

⅔ cup sugar
⅓ cup creamy peanut butter
1   cup dark corn syrup
½ teaspoon salt
3   eggs

1   cup salted peanuts
1   9-inch unbaked pie shell
1   (6-ounce) package semi-sweet
     chocolate chips

In mixing bowl, combine sugar, peanut butter, corn syrup, salt, and eggs, beating until smooth. Stir in peanuts. Pour into unbaked pie shell and sprinkle with chocolate chips. Bake at 375 degrees for 40 to 50 minutes. (Center of filling may be slightly soft but will become firm as pie cools). Cool 30 minutes. Refrigerate until chilled, at least 3 hours, but no longer than 24 hours.

NOTE: Anyone who enjoys peanuts will say this pie is a winner.

Butterscotch Pie

1   cup sugar
½ cup flour
½ cup butter, melted
2   eggs, slightly beaten
1   (6-ounce) package butterscotch
     chips

1   cup chopped pecans
1   teaspoon vanilla
1   9-inch unbaked pie shell

In bowl, mix together sugar and flour. Add melted butter, eggs, butterscotch chips, chopped pecans, and vanilla. Mix well. Pour mixture into an unbaked pie shell and bake at 325 degrees for 1 hour.

NOTE: Easy and very tasty.

Chocolate Crunch Pie

⅓ cup butter
⅓ cup light brown sugar
½ cup chopped pecans
1 9-inch pie shell
1 (6-serving) package vanilla pudding

1 (4-ounce) package German sweet chocolate, broken in pieces
2 cups milk
1 cup whipping cream, whipped

Combine butter, brown sugar, and pecans in saucepan. Heat until butter and sugar are melted. Watch carefully. Spread in bottom of pie shell. Bake at 450 degrees for 5 minutes or until bubbly. Cool. In another saucepan, combine pudding mix, chocolate, and milk. Cook and stir over medium heat until mixture comes to a full bubbling boil. Remove from heat. Pudding will thicken as it cools, stir occasionally. Pour into pie shell and cover with plastic wrap. Chill at least 4 hours. Remove plastic wrap and top with whipped cream. Refrigerate until serving.

Chocolate Chess Pie

1½ cups sugar
5 tablespoons cocoa
2 tablespoons flour
¼ teaspoon salt
½ cup evaporated milk

3 eggs, room temperature
⅓ cup unsalted butter, melted and cooled
1 teaspoon vanilla
1 9-inch unbaked pie shell

In large bowl, combine sugar, cocoa, flour, and salt and mix well, pressing out any lumps. Blend in milk. Beat in eggs, one at a time, beating well after each addition. Add butter and vanilla, beating until smooth. Pour filling into pie shell. Bake at 325 degrees until filling is puffed and set, 55 to 60 minutes. Let pie cool at room temperature before serving.

NOTE: Top this fudge-like pie with vanilla ice cream or whipped cream.

Fudge Pie

¼   **cup butter**
¾   **cup light brown sugar**
1   **(12-ounce) package semi-sweet**
    chocolate chips
3   **eggs, beaten**

¼   **cup flour**
1   **cup chopped pecans**
1   **teaspoon vanilla**
1   **9-inch unbaked pie shell**

In top of double boiler or in heavy saucepan, melt butter, brown sugar, and chocolate chips. Cool. Add beaten eggs. Combine flour with pecans and add to chocolate mixture. Stir in vanilla. Pour batter into pie shell. Bake at 375 degrees for 30 to 35 minutes. Let cool at room temperature before serving. Good with vanilla ice cream.

NOTE: A very rich chocolate pie — a chocolate lover's dream.

Chocolate Angel Pie

2   **egg whites**
⅛   **teaspoon salt**
⅛   **teaspoon cream of tartar**

½   **cup sugar**
½   **cup chopped pecans**
½   **teaspoon vanilla**

Beat egg whites until foamy. Add salt and cream of tartar. Continue beating until mixture forms soft peaks. Add sugar gradually and continue beating until very stiff. Do not underbeat. Fold in pecans and vanilla. Turn into lightly greased 8-inch pie plate, spreading up sides and covering bottom. Bake at 300 degrees for 55 minutes. Spread with Filling (see recipe below).

Filling:

1   **(4-ounce) package German**
    sweet chocolate
3   **tablespoons hot water**

1   **teaspoon vanilla**
1   **cup whipping cream, whipped**

Heat chocolate and water in microwave or saucepan over low heat until chocolate is melted; cool. Stir in vanilla. Beat whipping cream in chilled bowl until stiff. Fold chocolate into whipped cream. Spoon into meringue shell. Refrigerate until firm.

NOTE: A light chocolate pie.

Mocha Toffee Pie

1⅓ cups pie crust mix	1 teaspoon vanilla
¼ cup light brown sugar	1 tablespoon water
¾ cup finely chopped pecans	
1 (1-ounce) square unsweetened chocolate, grated	

Combine pie crust mix with brown sugar, pecans, and grated chocolate. Add vanilla and water. Blend with fork until combined. Turn into well buttered 9-inch pie plate. Press firmly against sides and bottom. Bake at 375 degrees for 15 minutes. Cool completely and fill with Chocolate Filling (see recipe below).

Chocolate Filling:

½ cup butter	1 teaspoon instant coffee, dissolved in 1 teaspoon water
¾ cup sugar	
1 (1-ounce) square unsweetened chocolate, melted and cooled	2 eggs

In mixing bowl, beat butter and sugar until light and creamy. Blend in cooled melted chocolate and coffee. Add 1 egg and beat 5 minutes. Add remaining egg and beat 5 minutes longer. Turn Filling into baked pie shell and refrigerate overnight. Next day, top with Topping (see recipe below).

Topping:

1 cup whipped cream	½ cup powdered sugar
1 teaspoon instant coffee	

In mixing bowl, combine whipping cream with coffee and powdered sugar. Beat until stiff peaks form. Spread on pie. Refrigerate at least 2 hours.

NOTE: This pie is rich and will be remembered.

German Chocolate Pie

1	(4-ounce) package German-sweet chocolate	2	tablespoons flour
½	cup butter	1	cup pecan halves
3	eggs	1	teaspoon vanilla
1	cup sugar	1	cup whipping cream, whipped

In top of a double boiler or in microwave, melt chocolate and butter. Set aside. In mixing bowl, beat eggs, sugar, and flour until well blended and light. Gradually add chocolate mixture, mixing well. Add pecans and vanilla. Pour into a buttered 9-inch pie plate. Bake at 350 degrees for 40 minutes. Filling will be soft, but it will set while cooling. Cool to room temperature and refrigerate until chilled. Top with whipped cream.

NOTE: This German Chocolate Pie is a real treat for chocolate lovers. It is easy to make and will definitely impress everyone!

Candies

Chocolate Nutty Fudge

2	cups sugar	¼	teaspoon salt
1	(5⅓-ounce) can evaporated milk	2	tablespoons butter
2	(1-ounce) squares unsweetened	1	teaspoon vanilla
	chocolate	1	cup coarsely chopped nuts
2	tablespoons light corn syrup		

In a 2-quart saucepan, heat sugar, milk, chocolate, corn syrup, and salt over medium heat, stirring constantly, until chocolate is melted and sugar is dissolved. Cook, stirring occasionally, to 234 degrees on candy thermometer or until small amount of mixture dropped into very cold water forms a soft ball which flattens when removed from water. Remove from heat; add butter and vanilla. Stir in pecans. Beat continuously with wooden spoon until candy is thick and no longer glossy (mixture will hold its shape when dropped from spoon). Quickly drop fudge into mounds on waxed paper. Let cool until firm. Yield: 20 candies.

NOTE: I like the fudge in individual pieces like this.

Special Fudge

1	cup butter	2	(16-ounce) boxes powdered
8	ounces pasteurized processed		sugar
	cheese spread	1	teaspoon vanilla
½	cup cocoa	1	cup chopped pecans

In saucepan, melt butter and cheese over low heat, watching carefully. Remove from heat. Blend in cocoa and powdered sugar until well mixed. Add vanilla and pecans. Place in a buttered 1½ quart oblong glass dish. Chill until hardened.

NOTE: You would never know about this secret ingredient unless told. It's very good.

Peanut Butter Fudge

1 (13½-ounce) can evaporated milk	1 cup butter
	1 cup peanut butter
4 cups sugar	1 cup marshmallow creme

In a heavy saucepan combine milk, sugar, and butter and cook over medium heat until reaches soft ball stage on candy thermometer. Remove from heat and add peanut butter and marshmallow creme. Pour into a 13×9×2-inch baking pan. Cool and cut into squares.

Mexican Fudge

3 cups sugar, divided	2 cups chopped pecans
1 cup scalded milk	¼ cup butter

In heavy saucepan, cook 1 cup of sugar until all is melted. Then slowly add scalded milk alternately with remaining 2 cups of sugar. Cook until mixture forms soft ball stage on candy thermometer. Add pecans and butter and beat until light in color and mixture sugars around edges of pot. Pour into a buttered 8×8×2-inch baking pan for thick squares.

Rocky Road Candy

2 cups peanuts	1 (14-ounce) can sweetened condensed milk
1 (10½-ounce) package miniature marshmallows	4 tablespoons butter
1 (12-ounce) package semi-sweet chocolate chips	1 teaspoon vanilla

Put wax paper in the bottom of a 13×9×2-inch baking pan. Grease well. Place peanuts and marshmallows evenly on bottom of pan. In saucepan, combine chocolate chips, milk, and butter, cooking over low heat until melted, stirring constantly. Remove from heat and add vanilla. Pour over marshmallow/peanut mixture in pan. Refrigerate for 2 hours.

Pralines

½ cup butter	2 cups chopped pecans
2 cups light brown sugar	2 teaspoons vanilla
½ cup milk	

Melt butter in heavy saucepan. Add brown sugar and milk. Cook until reaches soft ball stage in water or on candy thermometer. Remove from heat and add pecans and vanilla. Beat until creamy. Drop by spoonfuls onto waxed paper.

Peanut Patties

2½ cups sugar	3 cups peanuts
1 cup half-and-half cream	1 tablespoon butter
⅔ cup light corn syrup	1 teaspoon vanilla

Combine sugar, half-and-half, corn syrup, and peanuts in a heavy saucepan. Cook on medium high heat until soft ball forms in water or reaches soft ball stage on candy thermometer. Remove from heat. Add other ingredients and beat until mixture is thick and creamy. Drop by spoonfuls on waxed paper.

NOTE: These are like peanut pralines.

Turtles

1 (14-ounce) package caramels	2 cups chopped pecans
3 tablespoons sweetened condensed milk	1 (8-ounce) milk chocolate candy bar
1 teaspoon vanilla	½ bar paraffin

In microwave or in top of double boiler, melt caramels with sweetened condensed milk. Add vanilla and pecans. Drop by teaspoons onto buttered waxed paper. Let cool. In microwave or in top of double boiler, melt chocolate candy bar and paraffin. Use tongs and dip the caramels in the warm chocolate mixture and put back on the waxed paper to cool. Yield: 3 dozen turtles.

Sugared Pecans

1½ cups sugar
1 cup sour cream

1½ teaspoons vanilla
4 cups pecan halves

Combine all ingredients except pecans and vanilla in heavy saucepan. Cook over a medium heat, stirring constantly, and bring to soft ball stage on candy thermometer. Add vanilla and pecans and stir until dull in color and set. Pour out and spread on waxed paper and separate with forks. Cool.

NOTE: Put pecans in cute containers to give for gifts.

Chocolate Pretzels

1 (6-ounce) package semi-sweet chocolate chips
2 tablespoons light corn syrup

2 tablespoons shortening
1½ teaspoons water
24 (3-inch) twisted pretzels

Combine chocolate chips, corn syrup, shortening, and water in top of double boiler or in microwave, stirring frequently until mixture melts and is smooth. Remove from heat. Using 2 forks, dip each pretzel into chocolate mixture. Let chocolate drip from pretzels and then lay on racks with waxed paper underneath. Chill 10 minutes in refrigerator. Let stand at room temperature for 1 hour. Store in covered container. Yield: 2 dozen pretzels.

NOTE: This quick and easy recipe is a great holiday gift idea. It is easy to double. Also, can use fresh strawberries to dip in chocolate.

Thin Delights

48 thin square wheat crackers
½ cup crunchy peanut butter

4 cubes white almond bark

Lay 24 wheat crackers on waxed paper. Cover each with peanut butter and top with another wheat cracker to make a sandwich. In microwave or in top of double boiler, melt white almond bark. Ice top of each sandwich with melted white almond bark. Let sit on waxed paper until hardens.

NOTE: This unusual combination is so good it's like eating a candy bar.

Peanut Butter Balls

¾	cup butter, melted	2	cups graham cracker crumbs
1	(16-ounce) box powdered sugar	1	(12-ounce) package semi-sweet
2	cups crunchy peanut butter		chocolate chips
1	cup chopped pecans	½	bar paraffin wax

Combine all ingredients except chocolate chips and paraffin, mixing well. Roll into balls; lay balls on cookie sheet and freeze until ready to dip. Melt chocolate chips and ½ bar of wax in top of double boiler or in microwave. Stick toothpick into each ball and dip in chocolate, then place on wax paper until set. Yield: 8 dozen.

Butter Nut Candy

½	cup butter	1	(6-ounce) package semi-sweet
¾	cup light brown sugar		chocolate chips, melted
¾	cup chopped pecans or almonds		

Melt butter and brown sugar in a saucepan over low heat. Bring to a boil for 5 minutes. Sprinkle nuts over a buttered $9 \times 9 \times 2$-inch baking pan. Spread brown sugar mixture over nuts. Top with melted chocolate chips. Refrigerate. Yield: 1 pound candy.

Caramel Corn

8	cups popped popcorn	¼	teaspoon salt
¾	cup light brown sugar	¼	teaspoon baking soda
6	tablespoons butter	¼	teaspoon vanilla
3	tablespoons light corn syrup		

Spray cookie sheet with no-stick cooking spray and spread with popped popcorn. In small saucepan, combine sugar, butter, syrup, and salt and cook over medium heat until boiling; then cook for 5 minutes. Remove from heat and stir in baking soda and vanilla. Pour over popcorn and stir so all popcorn is covered. Bake at 300 degrees for 18 minutes. Remove from oven and stir. Return to oven and bake for 5 to 10 minutes. Place caramel corn in large bowl to cool. When cool, break apart. Store in airtight container.

Chocolate Nugget Bars

First Layer:

1 (12-ounce) package semi-sweet chocolate chips
½ cup butterscotch chips
½ cup creamy peanut butter

Melt all ingredients in microwave or in heavy saucepan. Stir well and spread half of mixture into a buttered 13×9×2-inch baking pan. Cool. Reserve other half of mixture for fourth layer. Top with Second Layer (see recipe below).

Second Layer:

1 cup sugar
¼ cup milk
4 tablespoons butter
¼ cup marshmallow creme
1 teaspoon vanilla
2 cups dry roasted peanuts

Bring sugar, milk, and butter to boil and boil for 5 minutes. Add marshmallow creme and vanilla. Pour over bottom layer and sprinkle with peanuts. Top with Third Layer (see recipe below).

Third Layer:

1 (14-ounce) bag caramels
2 tablespoons hot water

Add hot water to caramels and melt in saucepan or in microwave. Drizzle over peanuts and top with Fourth Layer (see recipe below).

Fourth Layer:

Spread reserved half of chocolate mixture on top. Cool completely and cut into squares. Refrigerate.

NOTE: Tastes like your favorite candy bar.

Chocolate Fruit Balls

¾ cup butter, room temperature
2 cups powdered sugar
½ teaspoon salt
3 cups flaked coconut, finely chopped
2 cups finely chopped pecans
1⅓ cups chopped candied pineapple

2 teaspoons hot coffee
2 teaspoons vanilla
2 teaspoons coffee liqueur
8 (1-ounce) squares semi-sweet chocolate
1 cup pecan halves

In mixing bowl, cream butter, sugar, and salt. Blend in coconut, 2 cups finely chopped pecans, and pineapple. Add coffee, vanilla, and coffee liqueur. Blend well. Chill mixture for 1 hour. Form into walnut-sized balls and place on cookie sheet. In top of double boiler or microwave, melt chocolate. Cover each ball with chocolate. Place pecan half on top of each ball. Refrigerate until set. Place in miniature candy cups to serve.

NOTE: Good to make around the holidays.

Fudgy Surprise Squares

1 (12-ounce) package peanut butter chips
1 (14-ounce) can sweetened condensed milk
2 teaspoons vanilla

¼ teaspoon salt
2 cups miniature marshmallows
¾ cup chopped pecans
2 (6-ounce) packages semi-sweet chocolate chips

Line 11×7×2-inch baking pan with foil, leaving slight overhang all around; butter foil. Melt peanut butter chips over low heat or in microwave. Remove from heat; stir in half the can of condensed milk, 1 teaspoon vanilla, and ⅛ teaspoon salt. Spread evenly in prepared pan; top with marshmallows and pecans, pressing lightly into candy layer. Melt chocolate chips over low heat or in microwave; remove from heat; add remaining condensed milk, 1 teaspoon vanilla, and ⅛ teaspoon salt and stir until smooth. Spread evenly over marshmallow/pecan layer, pressing lightly. Chill until firm. Cut candy into 1-inch squares; store in covered container. Yield: 3 pounds.

Divinity

2 cups sugar	2 egg whites
½ cup light corn syrup	1 cup chopped pecans
½ cup water	1 teaspoon vanilla

Combine sugar, corn syrup, and water in a saucepan. Cook until it forms a thin thread when dropped from a spoon or until it reaches 238 degrees on a candy thermometer. In a mixing bowl, beat egg whites until stiff. Then pour the hot syrup into the beaten egg whites, stirring constantly. Add pecans and vanilla. Beat until candy loses its shine. Drop on waxed paper.

Almond Roca

1½ cups finely chopped almonds, toasted	1 cup light brown sugar
½ cup butter	6 ounces milk chocolate candy bars, broken into pieces

Sprinkle ¾ cup toasted almonds on the bottom of a generously buttered 8 × 8 × 2-inch square baking pan. In medium saucepan, melt butter and brown sugar. Bring to a boil and cook, stirring until mixture reaches 300 degrees on a candy thermometer. Pour the hot syrup over the almonds. Spread with buttered spatula. Immediately top with milk chocolate candy. Spread the chocolate as it melts. Sprinkle remaining ¾ cup toasted almonds over the chocolate. Cool completely and break into small pieces.

Spectacular
Endings

Delicious Cheesecake

2 (8-ounce) packages cream cheese	1¼ cups graham cracker crumbs
1⅓ cups sugar	¼ cup sugar
3 cups sour cream	¼ cup chopped pecans
3 eggs	¼ teaspoon cinnamon
1 teaspoon vanilla	⅓ cup butter, melted
Dash salt	

In mixing bowl, cream together cream cheese and 1⅓ cups sugar until well blended. Add sour cream, mixing well. Add eggs, blending well. Add vanilla and salt. In another bowl, combine graham cracker crumbs, ¼ cup sugar, pecans, and cinnamon together. Add butter, stirring until well mixed. Pat crumb mixture in the bottom and slightly up the sides of a 10-inch springform pan. Pour batter over crumb crust. Bake at 375 degrees for 45 to 50 minutes or until cheesecake cracks around outer edges. Allow cheesecake to cool at room temperature and then refrigerate.

NOTE: Can top with your favorite topping if desired. Freezes well before adding topping. This is an outstanding plain cheesecake!

Black and White Cheesecake

20 chocolate sandwich creme cookies, crushed	3 (8-ounce) packages cream cheese
4 tablespoons butter, melted	1 cup sugar
10 ounces semi-sweet chocolate	6 eggs
1 cup whipping cream	3 teaspoons vanilla

Mix cookie crumbs and 3 tablespoons butter together in small bowl. Press into bottom of greased and floured 9-inch springform pan. Melt chocolate in top of double boiler or microwave. Stir remaining 1 tablespoon butter and ⅓ cup whipping cream into chocolate. In mixing bowl, beat cream cheese with sugar until light. Add eggs, one at a time, beating well after each. Add remaining ⅔ cup whipping cream and 2 teaspoons vanilla. Stir in 1½ cups of this filling into chocolate and spread over crust. Add last 1 teaspoon vanilla into remaining filling and pour carefully over chocolate layer. Place pan of hot water on lower oven rack. Bake cheesecake on middle rack at 300 degrees for 2 to 2½ hours. Cool to room temperature and refrigerate.

White Chocolate Cheesecake

Crust:

1 cup old fashioned oatmeal	1½ cups graham cracker crumbs
⅓ cup finely chopped slivered almonds	10 tablespoons unsalted butter, melted
¼ cup sugar	

Combine all ingredients in bowl except butter. Add butter, mixing well. Press mixture into bottom and up sides of a buttered 9-inch round springform pan. Bake at 350 degrees for 8 minutes. Cool and fill with White Chocolate Filling (see recipe below).

White Chocolate Filling:

3 (8-ounce) packages cream cheese	1 pound best quality white chocolate, melted
2 tablespoons sugar	
4 eggs	1 cup sour cream
½ cup butter, melted	1 tablespoon vanilla

In large mixing bowl, blend cream cheese and sugar until light and fluffy. Add eggs, one at a time, beating well after each addition. Add melted butter and melted white chocolate, combining well. Add sour cream and vanilla, mixing until well combined. Bake at 325 degrees for 55 minutes.

Praline Cheesecake

1   **cup graham cracker crumbs**   ¼   **cup butter, melted**
2   **tablespoons sugar**

Combine crumbs, sugar, and butter together in small bowl. Press evenly into bottom of a 9-inch springform pan. Top with Filling (see recipe below).

Filling:

3   **(8-ounce) packages cream cheese**   1½ **teaspoons vanilla**
1¼ **cups light brown sugar**   1   **cup chopped pecans**
3   **eggs**   ½   **cup caramel topping**
2   **tablespoons flour**

In mixing bowl, blend cream cheese and brown sugar until smooth. Add eggs, one at a time, beating well after each addition. Stir in flour, vanilla, and pecans. Reserve 1 cup batter and add caramel topping to it. Spoon half of plain batter over crust, cover with caramel batter, and spread remaining plain batter over top. Bake at 350 degrees for 55 minutes or until set. Let cheesecake cool to room temperature, cover and refrigerate. Pour Topping (see recipe below) over chilled cake, spreading to cover top.

Topping:

½   **cup light brown sugar**   **Pecan halves**
¼   **cup butter**

Combine brown sugar and butter in small saucepan. Place over low heat and cook, stirring occassionally, until smooth and thickened, about 5 minutes. Pour hot topping over chilled cake, spreading to cover top. Refrigerate until completely chilled. Remove rim of springform pan and arrange pecan halves decoratively around edge of topping.

NOTE: Always popular.

Pecan Praline Cheesecake

Crust:

1½ cups flour	1 cup butter, cut into pieces
¾ cup sugar	2 egg yolks

In bowl, mix flour and sugar. Cut in butter until mixture resembles coarse meal. Add yolks and mix until dough just begins to come together. Gather dough into ball; press into bottom of greased 10-inch springform pan. Bake at 375 degrees for 20 minutes, or until crust is golden brown. Cool slightly. Fill with Filling (see recipe below).

Filling:

1 cup sugar	1 teaspoon vanilla
1 cup light corn syrup	2 cups chopped pecans, toasted
3 eggs	

Blend sugar, corn syrup, eggs, and vanilla in large bowl. Mix in pecans. Pour filling over crust. Set springform pan on heavy baking sheet. Bake at 375 degrees until edges of filling are set but center remains soft, about 15 minutes. Cool while making Topping (see recipe below). Reduce oven temperature to 250 degrees.

Topping:

1 cup sugar	2 (8-ounce) packages cream
2 eggs, room temperature	cheese, room temperature, cut
1 teaspoon vanilla	into pieces
	1 cup fresh orange juice

In mixing bowl, blend sugar, eggs, and vanilla. Gradually add cream cheese and beat until smooth. Blend in orange juice. Pour over pecan filling. Bake at 250 degrees for about 1 hour and 50 minutes or until top of cake is golden brown and center remains firm when pan is moved. Cool completely in pan on rack. Cover and refrigerate overnight.

NOTE: A little different version — it is rich and worth the effort.

Truffle Tart

Nut Pastry:

1¼ cups flour
½ cup chopped pecans, toasted
2 tablespoons sugar
½ teaspoon salt

½ cup butter, cut into pieces
1½ tablespoons ice water
1 teaspoon vanilla

Combine first four ingredients in processor. Cut in butter until mixture resembles coarse meal. Combine water and vanilla; add to dry ingredients and process just until dough begins to gather together. Form dough into ball; flatten to disc. Wrap tightly and chill 30 minutes. Roll dough out on lightly floured surface to 12-inch diameter round. Transfer dough to 10 to 12-inch tart pan with 1-inch high removable sides. Trim and finish edges. Refrigerate at least 1 hour. (Can be prepared 1 day ahead). Bake at 350 degrees for 25 minutes. Spread with Ganache (see recipe below).

Ganache:

½ cup semi-sweet chocolate chips
2 tablespoons unsalted butter

½ cup whipping cream

Combine chocolate and butter in bowl. Scald cream. Add to chocolate mixture and let stand 5 minutes. Mix until chocolate melts and mixture is smooth. Pour into shallow pan. Cool. Cover and refrigerate at least 1 hour. (Ganache can be prepared 1 day ahead). Spread over bottom of tart shell. Cover with Pastry Cream (see recipe below).

Pastry Cream:

3 egg yolks
3 tablespoons sugar
3 tablespoons flour

1 cup milk
2 tablespoons unsalted butter
1 teaspoon vanilla

Whisk yolks and sugar in small bowl until light in color. Gradually mix in flour. Scald milk in heavy small saucepan. Gradually whisk into yolks. Return to saucepan. Boil 3 minutes, whisking constantly. Mix in butter and vanilla. Pour into small bowl. Cover and refrigerate until well chilled. (Can be prepared 1 day ahead). Top with Caramel Pecan Topping (see recipe next page).

Continued on next page

Caramel Pecan Topping:

¼ cup unsalted butter
½ cup light brown sugar
¼ cup sugar
½ cup whipping cream

½ teaspoon vanilla
1¼ cups coarsely chopped pecans,
   toasted

Melt butter in heavy saucepan over medium heat. Add both sugars and cook 5 minutes, stirring occassionally. Whisk in cream and vanilla; mixture will bubble up. Reduce heat to low and cook 5 minutes longer, stirring occassionally. Remove from heat and add pecans. Cool completely. Spread over pastry cream and refrigerate.

NOTE: A beautiful, rich tart that is well worth the effort.

Chocolate Pecan Torte

½ cup butter
2 cups flour
⅓ cup sugar
Dash salt
1 egg yolk, slightly beaten
1 teaspoon vanilla
½ tablespoon grated lemon rind
1 cup sugar

1 cup whipping cream, room
   temperature
3 tablespoons honey
2 tablespoons Grand Marnier
1¾ cups chopped pecans or walnuts
1 cup semi-sweet chocolate mini
   chips

In mixing bowl, cream butter until fluffy. Mix flour, ⅓ cup sugar, and dash salt together. Add to butter and beat until crumbly. Combine egg yolk, vanilla, and lemon rind; stir into flour until moistened. Pat dough onto bottom and up sides of a 10-inch springform pan. Chill crust. In skillet, melt 1 cup sugar over medium heat, stirring constantly, until golden. Remove from heat, slowly stir in cream. Heat and stir until sugar dissolves. Add honey, Grand Marnier and pecans. Remove from heat, cool to room temperature. Stir in mini chips, spread mixture in prepared pan. Bake at 350 degrees for 40 minutes. Remove from oven, cool completely.

NOTE: Definitely don't skip this delicious dessert.

Fruit Tart

2 cups flour	10 tablespoons butter
¼ cup sugar	1 egg yolk
Dash salt	4 tablespoons cold water
1 teaspoon vanilla	

In food processor or mixing bowl, combine flour, sugar, and salt. Add vanilla. Mix in butter with processor or with pastry blender until mixture forms coarse crumbs. Add egg yolk, combining well. Add water, mixing just until dough forms a ball. Refrigerate dough for 30 minutes. Roll out dough into an 11-inch circle and fit into a 10 to 11-inch tart pan. Cut parchment or waxed paper to fit bottom of pan. Fill with dried beans or rice. This will act as weights and prevent pie shell from shrinking and rising during baking. Bake at 375 degrees for 20 minutes. Remove rice and continue cooking 15 minutes longer or until pastry is golden. Cool pie shell and fill with Pastry Cream (see recipe below).

Pastry Cream:

½ cup cold milk	1½ cups hot milk
¼ cup cornstarch	½ cup sugar
4 egg yolks	1 teaspoon vanilla

In a heavy saucepan, mix ½ cup cold milk and cornstarch with a whisk. Add remaining ingredients, except vanilla. Cook over a low heat, stirring constantly with a wooden spoon, until mixture is very thick. Remove from heat and add vanilla. Chill until firm. Then fill cooled pastry with Pastry Cream. Cover with Fruit (see recipe below).

Fruit:

1 pint strawberries, stemmed and halved	1 kiwi, peeled and thinly sliced
	½ cup blueberries

Arrange strawberry halves, cut side down, in a roll in a circular pattern along outer edge of filled pastry. Next, place a roll of kiwi slices. Fill center with blueberries. Brush with Apricot Glaze (see recipe next page).

Continued on next page

Apricot Glaze:

1 cup apricot preserves	1 tablespoon lemon juice
1 tablespoon butter	2 tablespoons apricot brandy

In a small saucepan, mix all ingredients over low heat until hot. Cool and brush glaze on fruit with pastry brush or spoon gently over fruit. Best served same day made.

NOTE: This is a beautiful dessert, as well as delicious. Everyone will be impressed. Use your imagination and substitute different fruits.

Bread Pudding with Broiled Rum Topping

1 large loaf French bread, torn into pieces	2 cups sugar
	1 tablespoon vanilla
2 cups half-and-half cream	1 cup raisins
2 cups milk	¼ cup butter, melted
3 eggs, slightly beaten	

In bowl, soak bread with half-and-half and milk. Crush with hands until well mixed. Add eggs, sugar, vanilla, and raisins. Pour butter into bottom of a 13×9×2-inch baking pan. Pour bread pudding mixture into pan. Bake at 350 degrees for 50 minutes. Spoon Rum Sauce (see recipe below) on baked pudding.

Rum Sauce:

½ cup butter	1 egg
1 cup sugar	¼ cup rum

Cook butter and sugar in top of double boiler or in heavy saucepan until very hot and well dissolved. Then add well beaten egg and whip fast so egg does not curdle. Pour sauce over pudding and immediately run under broiler until brown and bubbly. Watch carefully.

NOTE: This is an outstanding bread pudding.

Amaretto Cheesecake

Crust:

1	(10-ounce) box shortbread cookies, ground fine	1	egg yolk (reserve white for filling)
¼	cup flour	2	tablespoons Amaretto
¼	cup sugar	½	cup slivered almonds, chopped
5	tablespoons unsalted butter		

Combine cookies, flour, and sugar. Add butter, mixing well. Mix in egg yolk and Amaretto. Reserve ⅓ cup mixture and add chopped almonds to remaining mixture. Grease a 9-inch springform pan and press almond crust mixture on bottom. Wrap pan with aluminum foil or place on a tray to prevent oils from dripping on bottom of oven. Bake at 350 degrees for 12 to 15 minutes until light brown. Remove from oven and place in freezer until cool. When pan is cool to the touch, regrease the sides and press remaining mixture against sides, bringing it all the way to the top. Pour Filling (see recipe below) into prepared pan.

Filling:

4	(8-ounce) packages cream cheese, softened	3	eggs, plus leftover egg white
1½	cups sugar	⅓	cup Amaretto
¼	cup flour	1	cup whipped cream

In mixing bowl, beat cream cheese and add sugar, ½ cup at a time, blending well until smooth. Add flour, blending well. Add eggs and reserved egg white, one at a time, blending well after each addition. Add Amaretto. Stir in whipped cream with a whisk until smooth. Pour into prepared crust. Place cheesecake in center of oven. Place a small pan of water on a lower rack. Bake at 350 degrees for 10 minutes. Then turn oven down to 250 degrees for 35 minutes. Turn oven off and allow cheesecake to cool in oven overnight or at least 4 hours without opening oven door. Refrigerate.

NOTE: Cheesecake is best if baked one night and served the following day.

Cobbler

3 to 4 cups fruit (peaches,	1¾ cups sugar
blueberries, or your choice)	½ cup butter, melted
2 tablespoons flour	

In bowl, combine all ingredients together and put into a 2-quart oblong baking dish. Top with Crust (see recipe below). Bake at 350 degrees for 45 minutes.

Crust:

2 cups flour	½ cup milk
1 teaspoon salt	½ cup butter, melted
⅔ cup shortening	Cinnamon and sugar

In small bowl, mix flour and salt. Cut in shortening with pastry blender. Mix in milk. Roll dough out on floured surface and cut into strips. Lay strips on top of fruit mixture. Pour ½ cup melted butter on top. Sprinkle dough with cinnamon and sugar. Bake at 350 degrees for 45 minutes.

NOTE: Don't let this homemade crust scare you. It's an easy dough to work with, and this is the best cobbler I've ever had.

Flan

8 tablespoons sugar	4 egg yolks or 3 whole eggs,
1 teaspoon water	beaten
2 cups milk	½ teaspoon vanilla

Place 6 tablespoons sugar and water in 8×8×2-inch baking glass dish. Heat over very low heat, shaking occasionally to prevent burning, until sugar turns into golden syrup. (You may heat in pot and pour into individual cups). Cool until firm. Combine milk, beaten yolks (or whole eggs), vanilla, and remaining 2 tablespoons sugar. Blend well and pour over caramel. Place in larger pan with water ½ inch. Bake at 325 degrees for 1 to 1½ hours until knife inserted in center comes out clean. Chill until serving. Invert cups to serve. Cut squares in pan before inverting.

Almond Custard

2 cups whipping cream	½ cup sugar
Dash cinnamon	1 egg, plus 5 egg yolks
½ cup ground blanched almonds	2 tablespoons brandy

In saucepan, combine cream and cinnamon and bring to a boil. Add almonds and sugar. In another bowl, beat egg and egg yolks together. Transfer to a saucepan. Place over low heat and add hot cream mixture, stirring constantly. Continue cooking and stirring until custard coats a spoon. Remove from heat. Stir in brandy. Pour custard into small pots or glass dishes and chill. Sprinkle cinnamon on top if desired. Yield: 6 servings.

Almond Cookie Tart

Crust:

½ cup butter, softened	½ teaspoon almond extract
½ cup light brown sugar	½ teaspoon vanilla
1 egg, beaten	½ cup finely chopped almonds,
1 cup flour	toasted
½ teaspoon baking powder	

In mixing bowl, combine all ingredients, beating until well blended. Press evenly into greased 10-inch springform pan with floured fingers. Bake at 350 degrees for 20 minutes or until set and begins to brown. Top with Almond Filling (see recipe below) and continue baking.

Almond Filling:

3 eggs	¼ teaspoon salt
1½ cups light brown sugar	½ teaspoon vanilla
¼ cup flour	1 teaspoon almond extract
1 teaspoon baking powder	2 cups chopped almonds, toasted

In large mixing bowl, combine all ingredients, mixing well. Pour Filling over hot crust and bake at 350 degrees for 35 to 40 minutes, until Filling is set. Cool to room temperature, remove from pan and chill.

NOTE: Can serve with dollop of whipped cream flavored with almond extract, if desired. This tart has a great flavor.

Almond Macaroon Cake

1 cup butter	2 cups crumbled almond
1 (16-ounce) box powdered sugar	macaroons
⅔ cup Amaretto	1 cup slivered almonds, toasted
5 egg yolks	1 (12-ounce) angel food cake

In mixing bowl, cream butter, powdered sugar, and Amaretto. Add egg yolks, one at a time, beating after each addition. Fold in macaroons and almonds. Slice cake into 4 layers. Spread mixture between layers. Refrigerate while making Frosting (see recipe below).

Frosting:

1 cup whipping cream	2 tablespoons Amaretto
¼ cup powdered sugar	½ cup slivered almonds, toasted

In mixing bowl, whip cream with sugar until stiff. Add Amaretto. Spread over cake and sprinkle with almonds. Refrigerate at least 30 minutes before serving.

NOTE: This cake is rich, wonderful and a conversation piece.

Fruit with Vanilla Sauce

2 pints half-and-half cream	¾ cup sugar
Half a vanilla bean or 1 teaspoon	5 egg yolks
vanilla	Fresh fruit

In a heavy saucepan or in the top of a double boiler, combine the half-and-half, vanilla bean, and sugar. Bring mixture to a boil, stirring constantly. In a mixing bowl, beat egg yolks until thick. Gradually add boiling cream mixture to beaten egg yolks, stirring constantly. Cool to room temperature and serve with fresh fruit.

NOTE: This is delicious as well as pretty. Fill parfait glasses with strawberries and blueberries and pour vanilla sauce on top.

Grand Marnier Soufflé

3	tablespoons butter	¼	cup Grand Marnier
3	tablespoons flour	1	teaspoon grated orange rind
1	cup warm milk	6	large egg whites, room
4	large egg yolks		temperature
⅓	cup sugar	1	tablespoon sugar
Pinch of salt			

Butter 2-quart soufflé dish and dust with powdered sugar; set aside. In medium saucepan, melt butter; stir in flour and cook 1 minute. Add milk and stir constantly over medium heat until thickened. Cool slightly. Beat egg yolks with ⅓ cup sugar and salt until thick. Stir in Grand Marnier and grated orange rind. Stir egg yolk mixture into milk mixture. Soufflé can be prepared up to this point two hours before serving. Beat egg whites with 1 tablespoon sugar until stiff and fold lightly into egg yolk mixture. Pile gently into prepared soufflé dish. Bake at 375 degrees for 25 to 30 minutes or until puffed and golden brown. Serve immediately with Creme Anglaise (see recipe below).

Creme Anglaise:

1¼	cups whipping cream		Pinch of salt
4	egg yolks	3	tablespoons Grand Marnier
½	cup sugar		

Heat cream in saucepan or microwave, but do not boil. In another saucepan, combine egg yolks, sugar, and salt, beating until light yellow in color. Add hot cream to egg yolk mixture and stir until blended. Cook over medium heat until sauce thickens, stirring with a wooden spoon. Cool. Add Grand Marnier just before serving.

Bananas Flambé

1	quart vanilla ice cream	¼	cup chopped pecans
1	cup butter	1	jigger banana liqueur
1	cup light brown sugar	1	jigger brandy flambé
⅛	teaspoon cinnamon		(can substitute rum)
4 to 6 bananas, peeled			

Mold ice cream into 6 balls and put back in freezer until ready to use. In a flambé pan or a large skillet, melt butter, brown sugar, and cinnamon over low heat. Slice bananas into long chunks on the diagonal. Add bananas and pecans and cook until bananas begin to turn soft. Drizzle the banana liqueur and brandy flambé and ignite. Be careful. Let flame for about one minute. When flame dies out, serve bananas and sauce on top of prepared ice cream balls. Yield: 6 servings.

NOTE: By making the ice cream balls ahead, it is great for entertaining. Also, the butter/brown sugar mixture can be made in advance and stored in the refrigerator. Reheat mixture, add bananas and pecans and follow directions.

Fantastic Trifle

1	(16-ounce) pound cake, cubed	3	cups whipping cream
1	(16-ounce) jar fudge topping	3	bananas, peeled and sliced
¼	cup coffee liqueur	1	(12-ounce) container whipped
6	(1³/₁₆-ounce) English toffee		topping
	candy bars, crushed		
3	(4-serving) packages instant		
	vanilla pudding		

Cube cake and put in bowl. Heat fudge and coffee liqueur in small saucepan or microwave. Pour fudge mixture over pound cake. Take five crushed toffee candy bars and add to pound cake mixture. Whisk pudding and whipping cream until thick (do not use mixer). Pour over pound cake mixture. Put in refrigerator for 30 minutes. In a trifle dish, layer pound cake mixture, banana, and whipped topping. Repeat the layers, ending with whipped topping on top. Crush the remaining toffee candy bar on top.

NOTE: This is an easy but spectacular dessert. Make the night before.

Chocolate Trifle

Cream Filling:

7 (1-ounce) squares semi-sweet chocolate	1 egg yolk, beaten
	1 teaspoon vanilla
1 (8-ounce) package cream cheese, softened	2 egg whites, room temperature
	1/4 cup sugar
1/4 cup sugar	1 cup whipping cream, whipped

In top of double boiler or in microwave, melt chocolate. In small bowl, beat together cream cheese, 1/4 cup sugar, and egg yolk until smooth. Add to chocolate, stirring until well mixed. Stir in vanilla and remove from heat; cool. In large bowl, beat egg whites until soft peaks form. Gradually add 1/4 cup sugar, beating until stiff peaks form. Fold in cooled chocolate mixture. Fold in whipped cream. Chill in covered bowl overnight.

Cake:

1 1/3 cups flour	1 teaspoon vanilla
1 cup sugar	3/4 cup raspberry preserves
3 tablespoons cocoa	1/4 cup sherry
1/2 teaspoon baking soda	1 cup whipping cream
1/2 teaspoon salt	1 tablespoon sugar
1 egg	1/2 teaspoon vanilla
1/3 cup oil	1/4 cup sliced almonds, toasted
3/4 cup water	1/2 cup fresh raspberries

Sift together flour, 1 cup sugar, cocoa, baking soda, and salt. Add egg, oil, water, and vanilla. Beat until well blended, about 2 minutes. Pour into greased and floured 8 × 8 × 2-inch square baking pan. Bake at 350 degrees for 30 to 35 minutes or until wooden pick inserted in center comes out clean. Cool in pan for 10 minutes. Turn out onto rack and let cool completely. Split cake in half horizontally and spread preserves on bottom. Replace top of cake and pierce cake all over with fork. Drizzle sherry evenly over cake. Cut into 1-inch squares and set aside.

Continued on next page

In a trifle dish or a glass bowl, put ½ cup cream filling in bottom. Top with ⅓ cake cubes. Repeat with two more layers of cream filling and cake. Cover with plastic wrap. Chill at least 3 hours, or up to 3 days. Whip 1 cup whipping cream with sugar and vanilla until soft peaks form. Cover top of trifle with whipped cream. Decorate top with toasted almonds and fresh raspberries.

NOTE: This spectacular dessert is better made ahead, which gives you more time. However, if in a pinch, substitute a pound cake for the homemade cake. It will be a hit either way.

Trifle

¾	cup sugar	½	cup sherry
⅓	cup cornstarch	1	pound strawberries, stemmed and sliced
⅛	teaspoon salt		
3	cups milk	2	bananas, peeled and sliced
4	egg yolks, slightly beaten	1	pint blueberries
1	teaspoon vanilla	2	kiwis, peeled and sliced
1	(16-ounce) pound cake, cut into ½-inch slices	1	cup whipping cream
		2	tablespoons powdered sugar

In a 2-quart saucepan, stir together sugar, cornstarch, and salt. Gradually add milk, stirring until smooth. Stir in beaten egg yolks. Cook over low heat, stirring constantly, until mixture comes to a boil. Boil 1 minute and remove from heat. Stir in vanilla. Cover with waxed paper and refrigerate until chilled. Arrange half of pound cake slices in single layer in trifle dish or other deep glass bowl. Sprinkle with ¼ cup sherry. Layer with half of fruit. Spoon half of custard over fruit. Repeat layering with remaining ingredients, beginning with pound cake. Whip cream in bowl until soft peaks form. Add powdered sugar and continue beating until stiff. Spoon whipped cream on top of trifle. Chill until ready to serve.

NOTE: This is a spectacular presentation.

Chocolate Mousse Cake

2	cups flour	Dash salt	
2	cups sugar	1	cup water
½	cup buttermilk	½	cup butter
1	teaspoon baking soda	1	cup shortening
2	eggs	4	tablespoons cocoa
1	teaspoon vanilla		

Sift flour and sugar in a large bowl. Add buttermilk, baking soda, eggs, vanilla, and salt. Combine water, butter, shortening, and cocoa in a saucepan and bring to a boil. Add to flour mixture, mixing well. Pour batter into three greased and floured 9-inch round cake pans. Bake at 350 degrees for 20 to 25 minutes or until cake springs back to the touch. Ice cake with Chocolate Mousse Frosting (see recipe below).

Chocolate Mousse Frosting:

5	(1-ounce) squares semi-sweet chocolate	5	eggs, separated
2	tablespoons water	¼	cup sugar
2	tablespoons cocoa	1	cup whipping cream

Combine chocolate, water, and cocoa in top of double boiler or in microwave. Cook, stirring until chocolate is melted and mixture is smooth. Remove from heat. Add egg yolks, one at a time, beating constantly after each addition. Set aside. In mixing bowl, beat egg whites until stiff, adding sugar gradually. Fold into chocolate mixture. Whip cream until soft peaks form and fold into chocolate mixture. Spread between layers and over cooled cake. Store cake covered in refrigerator.

NOTE: Do not pass this cake by — it is fabulous.

Chocolate Mousse in
White Chocolate Baskets

12 ounces white chocolate	1 tablespoon coffee cream liqueur
3 (1-ounce) squares unsweetened	or coffee liqueur
chocolate	1 teaspoon vanilla
3 tablespoons water	3 egg whites
½ cup sugar	1 cup whipping cream
3 egg yolks, beaten	

Melt white chocolate in top of double boiler. Stir until smooth. Spoon small amount of melted white chocolate into 12 paper muffin cup liners. Using back of spoon, smooth chocolate on bottom and up sides of liners. Set in muffin tins. Refrigerate until firm. Meanwhile, in top of double boiler or in small heavy saucepan over low heat, melt unsweetened chocolate in the water. Add sugar, stirring constantly. The mixture will be thick. Add egg yolks, stirring constantly, blending well. Remove from heat. Add liqueur and vanilla. In mixing bowl, beat egg whites until stiff. Fold beaten egg whites into chocolate mixture. In another chilled bowl, beat whipping cream until stiff. Fold into chocolate mixture. Carefully peel paper from white chocolate cups. Set on serving tray. Fill with chocolate mousse. Refrigerate until firm. Yield: 12 baskets filled with mousse.

Chocolate Ice Box Cake

2 (4-ounce) packages German sweet chocolate	2 dozen Lady Fingers
¼ cup butter	1 (7-ounce) jar marshmallow creme
⅓ cup powdered sugar	½ cup chopped pecans
4 eggs, separated	1 cup whipping cream, whipped
1 teaspoon vanilla	

In top of double boiler or in heavy saucepan, combine chocolate, butter, and powdered sugar, stirring until melted. In small bowl, beat egg yolks until light. Gradually add to chocolate mixture, stirring constantly for 1 minute. Remove from heat and add vanilla. Set aside to cool. Line sides and bottom of a 9-inch springform pan with Lady Fingers, split lengthwise. Spread marshmallow creme over Lady Fingers on bottom. Sprinkle with pecans. In mixing bowl, beat egg whites until stiff. Fold into chocolate mixture. Pour chocolate mixture over pecans. Refrigerate overnight, or at least 6 hours before serving. Top with whipped cream. Freezes well.

NOTE: Excellent.

Chocolate Divine Dessert

⅔ cup slivered almonds	3 egg whites, stiffly beaten
1 (12-ounce) package semi-sweet chocolate chips	2 cups whipping cream, whipped
3 tablespoons sugar	1 teaspoon vanilla
3 egg yolks, beaten	1 (8-ounce) angel food cake
	¼ cup coffee liqueur

Place almonds on ungreased cookie sheet and bake at 350 degrees until light golden brown. Watch carefully so almonds do not burn. Cool and set aside. In top of double boiler, melt chocolate chips with sugar. Cool. Mix in beaten egg yolks. Gradually fold in stiffly beaten egg whites. Fold in whipped cream and vanilla. Tear up angel food cake into ½-inch pieces. Put half of cake pieces on bottom of buttered 10-inch springform pan. Drizzle half of the coffee liqueur over the cake pieces. Cover with half of chocolate mixture. Layer remaining cake, liqueur, and chocolate. Refrigerate at least 24 hours. Remove springform rim. Top with toasted almonds. May be made up to three days in advance.

NOTE: This dessert is as the name says: divine.

Chocolate Yule Log

¼ cup butter	⅓ cup cocoa
1 cup chopped pecans	⅔ cup flour
1½ cups flaked coconut	¼ teaspoon salt
1 (14-ounce) can sweetened condensed milk	¼ teaspoon baking soda
	⅓ cup water
3 eggs	1 teaspoon vanilla
1 cup sugar	Powdered sugar

Line a 15 × 10 × 1-inch jelly roll pan with foil. Melt butter in jelly roll pan. Sprinkle pecans and coconut evenly in pan. Drizzle with condensed milk and set aside. In a mixing bowl, beat eggs on high speed until fluffy. Gradually add sugar and continue beating for 2 minutes. Combine cocoa, flour, salt, and baking soda. Add dry ingredients, water, and vanilla; blend well. Pour evenly into prepared pan. Bake at 350 degrees for 20 to 25 minutes until cake springs back when touched. Do not overcook. While cake is in pan, sprinkle with powdered sugar. Cover with a large clean towel. Invert pan so cake will turn out onto towel. Remove foil. Roll up cake immediately and re-cover with foil to hold together. When cool, place on a serving platter and frost with Chocolate Icing (see recipe below). Frost both ends, as well as a few lengthwise swirls to resemble bark on a log. If desired, place holiday greenery on a platter for color.

Chocolate Icing:

¼ cup butter	1 (16-ounce) box powdered sugar
⅓ cup cocoa	Milk to spread

In mixing bowl, combine butter, cocoa, and powdered sugar. Gradually add enough milk to make spreading consistency.

NOTE: This dessert will leave an impression with your guests — good for holidays.

143

Tortoni

1 egg white	1/8 teaspoon almond extract
1/4 teaspoon salt	1/4 cup chopped almonds, toasted
4 tablespoons powdered sugar	1 teaspoon shortening
1 cup whipping cream	1/2 cup semi-sweet chocolate pieces
1 teaspoon vanilla	

In mixing bowl, beat egg white and salt until stiff. Gradually add 2 tablespoons powdered sugar. In another bowl, beat whipping cream, remaining 2 tablespoons powdered sugar, vanilla, and almond extract until stiff. Fold both mixtures together. Put in freezer until mixture begins to freeze. Fold in toasted almonds. In top of double boiler or microwave, melt shortening and chocolate. Drizzle melted chocolate into chilled mixture and stir until mixed. This chips chocolate. Pour mixture in champagne glasses or 2-ounce paper cups in muffin pans and keep in freezer until ready to serve. Yield: 4 to 6 servings.

NOTE: This light dessert is great after an Italian dinner.

Frozen Filled Oranges

8 small naval oranges	1¾ cups sugar
1/2 cup butter	3 eggs, separated
Grated rind of 1 lemon	1 cup whipping cream
1/3 cup lemon juice	1 teaspoon cream of tartar
1/4 teaspoon salt	

Remove a 1-inch slice from top of each orange. Scoop out pulp and discard. Place shells in freezer. In top of double boiler, whisk butter, lemon rind, lemon juice, salt, 1½ cups sugar, and egg yolks. Cook, stirring, until thick. Cool. Whip cream until stiff. Fold into lemon mixture. Cover and freeze for 4 hours. Before serving, beat egg whites with cream of tartar until soft peaks form. Gradually add ¼ cup sugar, beating until stiff peaks form. To serve: fill orange shells two-thirds full with lemon mixture. Spread meringue on top. Broil until lightly browned, about 15 to 25 seconds. Watch very carefully. Serve immediately.

Ice Cream Sandwiches

1	cup shortening	⅓	cup cocoa
1	cup sugar	1	teaspoon baking soda
½	cup light brown sugar	½	teaspoon salt
2	eggs	1	cup semi-sweet chocolate mini
1	teaspoon vanilla		chips
2	cups flour		Vanilla ice cream

In large mixing bowl, cream shortening, sugar, brown sugar, eggs, and vanilla until light and fluffy. Combine flour, cocoa, baking soda, and salt, and add to creamed mixture. Stir in mini chips. Drop by heaping tablespoons onto ungreased baking sheet. Flatten each with palm of hand (4-inch circle) ¼-inch thick. Bake at 375 degrees 8 to 10 minutes or until almost set. Cool 1 minute on cookie sheet and then remove to wire rack to cool completely. Place scoop of slightly softened vanilla ice cream on flat side of 1 cookie, spread evenly with spatula, top with second cookie, pressing lightly. Wrap immediately in plastic wrap and freeze until firm. Yield: Approximately 12 ice cream sandwiches.

NOTE: Good to always have in your freezer when you want an ice cream treat.

Homemade Vanilla Ice Cream

2	cups milk	4	egg yolks
½	cup sugar	1	tablespoon vanilla
	Dash salt	1	cup whipping cream

In heavy saucepan, combine the milk, sugar, salt, and egg yolks. Cook over low heat, stirring constantly, until the mixture has thickened. *Cook slowly.* There may be lumps in mixture, but they will disappear when ice cream is freezing. Cool and add vanilla. Stir in whipping cream. Freeze according to directions of ice cream maker. Yield: 1 quart.

NOTE: Can add to this recipe to make different flavors.

Ice Cream Split Dessert

1 *(12-ounce) box vanilla wafers, crushed*	1 *(12-ounce) can evaporated milk*
¼ *cup butter, melted*	1 *(6-ounce) package semi-sweet chocolate chips*
3 *large bananas, peeled and sliced*	2 *cups powdered sugar*
½ *gallon Neapolitan ice cream, softened*	1 *teaspoon vanilla*
1 *cup chopped pecans*	2 *cups whipping cream*
½ *cup butter*	3 *tablespoons sugar*

In bowl, combine crushed vanilla wafers and ¼ cup butter and press in bottom of a 13×9×2-inch dish. Then top with a layer of sliced bananas. Cover bananas with ice cream and then sprinkle with pecans. Freeze overnight. Make a chocolate sauce by combining ½ cup butter, evaporated milk, chocolate chips, powdered sugar and vanilla in saucepan. Cook over low heat, stirring until mixture is pudding consistency. Chill pudding and pour ⅔ of pudding over frozen mixture. Whip cream until soft peak forms. Gradually add 3 tablespoons sugar and whip until stiff. Top chocolate pudding with whipped cream and drizzle with remaining chocolate. Freeze until serving time. Yield: 12 to 14 servings.

NOTE: A sensational ice cream dessert. Easy and can be made ahead!

Lemon Ribbon Ice Cream Pie

Lemon Butter Sauce:

6	tablespoons butter	2	eggs
	Grated rind of 1 lemon	2	egg yolks
⅓	cup lemon juice	1	quart vanilla ice cream
⅛	teaspoon salt	1	9-inch baked pie crust
1	cup sugar		

In heavy saucepan or in top of double boiler, melt butter over low heat. Add lemon rind, lemon juice, salt, and sugar, cooking until sugar is dissolved. Slightly beat whole eggs with egg yolks in small bowl. Gradually add a little of the lemon mixture to the beaten eggs and then add it all back to mixture in pan. Cook, beating constantly with a whisk until thick and smooth. Cool. Then, smooth half of the ice cream into the baked pie shell; freeze. Spread over it half the cooled lemon butter; freeze. Cover with the other half of the ice cream; freeze. Top with remaining lemon butter; freeze. Serve with Raspberry Sauce (see recipe below).

Raspberry Sauce:

2	(10-ounce) packages frozen raspberries in syrup, thawed	¼	cup sugar
			2 to 3 tablespoons Grand Marnier

Drain 1 package raspberries and discard juice. Save juice from other package. Purée fruit, juice, sugar, and liqueur in food processor or blender; strain purée to remove seeds. Chill until ready to use. Yield: 1½ cups sauce. (Freezes well). Raspberry Sauce can be used for other things, too.

NOTE: This is easy and elegant. It is a cool, refreshing dessert.

Mocha Meringue Pie

3   egg whites, room temperature
½   teaspoon baking powder
¾   cup sugar
Pinch of salt
1   cup chocolate sandwich creme
     cookies, crushed
½   cup chopped pecans

1   teaspoon vanilla
1   quart coffee ice cream, softened
1   cup whipping cream
½   cup powdered sugar
Chocolate curls, if desired
½ to ⅔ cup coffee liqueur

In mixing bowl, beat egg whites until frothy; add baking powder, beating slightly. Gradually add sugar and salt; continue beating until stiff and glossy. Fold in chocolate cookie crumbs, pecans, and vanilla. Spoon meringue mixture into a buttered 9-inch pie plate; use spoon to shape meringue into a pie shell, swirling sides high. Bake at 350 degrees for 30 minutes; cool. Spread ice cream evenly over meringue crust; cover and freeze overnight. In mixing bowl, beat whipping cream and powdered sugar until light and fluffy; spread on pie. Garnish with chocolate curls, if desired. Freeze until firm. Let pie stand at room temperature 10 minutes before slicing. Pour 1 tablespoon coffee liqueur over each serving.

NOTE: This pie is thick, rich and can be made ahead of time.

Deluxe Mocha Pie

Crust:

½ cup butter, softened   1 cup flour
2 tablespoons sugar

In small bowl, mix butter and sugar until light and fluffy. Add flour, stirring until mixture resembles coarse meal. Press onto bottom and sides of buttered 9-inch deep pie plate. Bake at 375 degrees for 12 to 15 minutes or until light golden brown; cool. Spoon Filling (see recipe below) into baked crust.

Filling:

⅓ cup chopped pecans	1 egg white, room temperature
1 (6-ounce) package semi-sweet	1 teaspoon instant coffee granules
chocolate chips	1 teaspoon vanilla
¼ cup light corn syrup	1½ cups whipping cream, whipped
¼ cup water	3 tablespoons Hot Fudge Sauce,
½ cup sugar	warmed
¼ cup water	

Place chopped pecans on cookie sheet and toast at 375 degrees for 5 to 7 minutes, watching carefully. Cool. In small saucepan, stir chocolate chips, corn syrup, and ¼ cup water over low heat until chips melt; cool. In large bowl, beat sugar, ¼ cup water, egg white, coffee granules, and vanilla until soft peaks form. Fold chocolate mixture, whipped cream, and pecans into egg white mixture. Spoon into baked crust. Decorate top with warmed Hot Fudge Sauce by drizzling chocolate in 3 concentric circles; pull knife tip from center to edge in several places to create web design. Sprinkle top with reserved toasted crumbs. Freeze until firm, about 4 to 6 hours. Cover if stored longer. Let sit at room temperature before serving.

NOTE: This pie has the consistency of chocolate mousse. It is pretty to serve and tastes fabulous.

Chocolate Almond Torte with Hazelnut Fudge Sauce

Chocolate Wafer Crust:

2 cups chocolate wafer cookie crumbs	4 tablespoons butter, melted

In small bowl or food processor, blend cookie crumbs and butter. Press into bottom of an 9-inch springform pan. Fill crust with Filling (see recipe below).

Filling:

4 egg whites	1 tablespoon vanilla
Dash salt	8 (1-ounce) squares semi-sweet chocolate
Dash cream of tartar	
¼ cup sugar	¾ cup chopped almonds, toasted
2 cups whipping cream	

In large mixing bowl, beat egg whites until frothy. Add salt and cream of tartar and beat until soft peak forms. Add the sugar, 1 tablespoon at a time, beating well after each addition. Transfer mixture to a large bowl that can be put in the freezer. In same mixing bowl, beat the cream and vanilla until stiff. Fold cream into whites and place bowl uncovered in freezer until top is almost solid and icy, and underneath the mixture is very cold but not frozen, approximately 1 hour. In top of double boiler or in microwave, melt chocolate. Add almonds. While the mixture is hot, quickly fold it into the very cold cream mixture. Small chunks of chocolate slivers will form when the hot mixture hits the cold. Pour into crust, cover tightly with foil, and freeze until solid. Serve with warm Hazelnut Fudge Sauce (see recipe below). Let sit at room temperature before serving.

Hazelnut Fudge Sauce:

7 (1-ounce) imported milk chocolate bars with hazelnuts, chopped	½ cup evaporated milk

In top of double boiler or in microwave, melt chocolate bars and ¼ cup evaporated milk. When melted, stir in as much evaporated milk as needed to obtain desired consistency.

Chocolate Fondue

16 ounces semi-sweet chocolate
2 tablespoons butter
½ cup sugar
1 cup whipping cream

1 teaspoon vanilla
2 tablespoons Cointreau
1 cup finely chopped almonds, toasted

Melt chocolate and butter in top of double boiler or in heavy saucepan. Blend in sugar and cream. Add vanilla and Cointreau. Fold in chopped almonds. Serve with fresh fruit or cubes of cake. Can make ahead and keep in refrigerator.

NOTE: This is so good and a nice dessert to have at a cocktail party.

White Chocolate Mousse

1½ cups sugar
¾ cup water
Dash cream of tartar
18 ounces white chocolate, finely chopped

7 egg whites
4 cups whipping cream, whipped
⅔ cup Grand Marnier

In saucepan, combine sugar, water, and cream of tartar. Bring to a boil and cook, stirring, until mixture reaches 230 degrees on candy thermometer. Before sugar mixture is ready, beat egg whites in bowl until stiff. When sugar mixture is ready, gradually add to beaten egg whites, folding until well mixed. Fold in white chocolate. Place mixture in freezer until *well chilled!* Combine whipped cream and Grand Marnier and fold into cold white chocolate mixture. Return to freezer. Cover. Freeze at least 1 hour prior to serving. Stays in freezer up to 2 weeks. Mousse has ice creamy consistency. Yield: 1 gallon.

NOTE: This sensational mousse is even better served with Raspberry Sauce (page 147).

Boston Cream Pie

¾	cup butter	3	cups flour
1½	cups sugar	2½	teaspoons baking powder
3	eggs	½	teaspoon salt
1	teaspoon vanilla	1	cup milk

In mixing bowl, beat butter and sugar until light and fluffy. Add eggs, beating well. Add vanilla. Combine flour, baking powder, and salt together. Add alternately with milk to creamed mixture, beginning and ending with dry ingredients. Pour batter into two greased and floured 9-inch round cake pans. Bake at 350 degrees for 25 minutes. Cool in pan 10 minutes and invert to cooling racks. After cooled completely, split each layer in half and fill with Cream Filling (see recipe below).

Cream Filling:

1	cup sugar	3	eggs, beaten
⅔	cups flour	4	tablespoons butter
½	teaspoon salt	2	teaspoons vanilla
3½	cups milk		

While cake is baking, prepare Filling. In heavy saucepan, combine sugar, flour, salt, and milk. Cook until mixture thickens and comes to a boil, stirring constantly. Cook another 2 minutes. Pour some of hot custard into beaten eggs and return to remaining custard in pan. Heat to boiling. Remove from heat and add butter and vanilla. Pour into a bowl, cover and refrigerate until chilled. Spread between split layers and ice top of cake with Chocolate Glaze (see recipe below).

Chocolate Glaze:

2	tablespoons butter	1	cup powdered sugar
1	(1-ounce) square unsweetened	2	tablespoons boiling water
	chocolate	½	tablespoon vanilla

In microwave or in top of double boiler, melt butter and chocolate. Stir in powdered sugar, water, and vanilla. Cover top of cake and let drip down sides.

NOTE: A fabulous cake full of custard with a touch of chocolate.

Lemon Crepe Dessert

Crepes:

2   cups flour
2   tablespoons powdered sugar
Dash salt
5   eggs

2   cups milk
2   tablespoons brandy
Butter

Sift flour with powdered sugar and salt. In mixing bowl, beat eggs and add dry ingredients, stirring until smooth. Gradually add milk and brandy. Beat well. Brush crepe pan with butter and heat. Pour in 2 tablespoons batter and tilt pan to spread evenly. Brown quickly on each side. Remove to waxed paper to cool. Yield: 16 crepes. Prepare Topping (see recipe below).

Topping:

½   cup sugar
2   teaspoons grated lemon rind
¾   cup butter
¼   cup cognac

¼   cup Cointreau
2   tablespoons lemon juice
⅓   cup sliced almonds, toasted

Fold the crepes in half and arrange one layer overlapping slightly in a buttered shallow baking dish. Sprinkle crepes with combined sugar and grated lemon rind. Dot with 2 tablespoons butter. Broil the crepes about 5 inches from heat until sugar is melted and bubbly. In a saucepan, melt remaining butter. Add cognac, Cointreau and lemon juice. Heat, stirring until blended. Sprinkle the almonds over the crepes and serve with sauce. Yield: 8 servings.

Trim &
Terrific

Almond Crescents

1 cup margarine	½ teaspoon almond extract
⅓ cup sugar	1⅔ cups flour
⅔ cup finely chopped almonds	½ cup powdered sugar

In mixing bowl, combine margarine, sugar, almonds, and almond extract. Mix in flour. Chill dough for 2 hours. Roll dough into the shape of a thin crescent. Bake at 325 degrees for 15 minutes on ungreased baking sheet. Cool a few minutes and dip warm crescent in powdered sugar. Yield: 48 crescents.

Calories: 69 Fat: 4.8 g. Cholesterol: 0 mg.

Almond Meringues

2 egg whites	⅓ cup sugar
¼ teaspoon cream of tartar	½ teaspoon grated orange rind
1 teaspoon almond extract	⅔ cup chopped almonds, toasted

In mixing bowl, beat egg whites with cream of tartar until frothy. Add almond extract. Gradually add sugar, beating constantly until stiff peaks are glossy. Fold in orange rind and almonds. Drop by spoonfuls onto cookie sheet lined with parchment. Bake at 275 degrees for 45 minutes. Yield: 16 meringues.

Calories: 48 Fat: 2.8 g. Cholesterol: 0 mg.

Lemon Sours

Here's a great lemon bar cookie that is perfect for any occasion.

1 cup flour	1 cup light brown sugar
2 tablespoons sugar	1 tablespoon lemon juice
4 tablespoons margarine	1 teaspoon lemon rind
2 large eggs	Lemon Glaze (recipe follows)

Preheat the oven to 350 degrees. In a bowl, combine the flour and sugar. Cut in the margarine with a pastry blender or fork until mixture resembles coarse meal. Press into an ungreased 9-inch square pan. Bake for 13 to 15 minutes or until light brown. In a mixing bowl, beat together the eggs, brown sugar, lemon juice, and lemon

Continued on next page

rind until well mixed and light. Spread over the baked crust. Return to the oven and continue baking for 20 minutes longer or until top is browned and puffed. Loosen edges around the pan while warm. Top with Lemon Glaze while hot. Cool and cut into squares. Yield: 25 squares.

Lemon Glaze:

1 tablespoon lemon juice	*1 teaspoon grated lemon rind*
⅔ cup powdered sugar	

Stir lemon juice into powdered sugar; blending until smooth. Add lemon rind and mix well. Spread on sours while warm.

Calories: 90   Cholesterol: 17 mg.   Fat: 2.3 g.   Fat Calories: 22%

Sweet Potato Cheesecake

The dark brown sugar and praline liqueur combined with the nutritiously wonderfully flavored yam makes this a sensational choice. Here's my Louisiana touch to cheesecake. Canned yams can be used also.

2 (8-ounce) packages light cream cheese	*2 large egg whites*
1 cup nonfat sour cream	*2 tablespoons praline liqueur or liqueur of choice*
1 cup mashed, cooked sweet potatoes (yams)	*2 teaspoons vanilla extract*
1 cup dark brown sugar	*1 (9-inch) prepared low-fat graham cracker crust*
1 large egg	

Preheat the oven to 350 degrees. In a large mixing bowl, beat together the cream cheese and sour cream until creamy. Add the sweet potatoes and brown sugar. Add the egg and egg whites one at a time, beating well after each addition. Add the praline liqueur and vanilla. Spoon the mixture into the prepared graham cracker crust. Bake for 40 to 50 minutes or until set. Remove from the oven to cool. Refrigerate until chilled, about 2 hours. Yield: 8 servings.

NOTE: To make your own crust. Mix together 1 cup graham cracker crumbs, 2 tablespoons sugar and 2 tablespoons margarine with a fork. Put into bottom and sides of pan.

Calories: 442   Cholesterol: 61 mg.   Fat: 13.7 g.   Fat Calories: 28%

Chocolate Almond Cheesecake

Cheesecake fans can indulge themselves with this rich tasting favorite version of America's favorite dessert.

½ cup chocolate wafer crumbs
1 (8-ounce) package fat-free cream cheese
1 (8-ounce) package reduced fat cream cheese
1 cup sugar

1½ cups fat-free cottage cheese, puréed in food processor until smooth
1 large egg
1 teaspoon vanilla extract
¼ cup flour
¼ cup cocoa
⅓ cup almond liqueur

Preheat the oven to 325 degrees. Spread the chocolate crumbs on the bottom of a 9-inch springform pan; set aside. In a mixing bowl, beat together the cream cheeses, sugar, cottage cheese, egg, and vanilla. Mix together the flour and cocoa and gradually add to cream cheese mixture. Add almond liqueur. Pour batter into the pan and bake for one hour. Remove from oven, cool to room temperature, and refrigerate until well chilled. Remove the sides of the pan and serve. Yield: 12 servings.

Calories: 214   Cholesterol: 33 mg.   Fat: 4.8 g.   Fat Calories: 20%

Heavenly Cheesecake

There's always those who prefer a plain cheesecake. For an added attraction, just open a can of fruit pie filling (blueberry, cherry…) and spread over the top and you'll have a winner with this rich and creamy delicious cheesecake.

1 cup crushed graham cracker crumbs
1 tablespoon sugar
2 tablespoons water
1 cup sugar
¼ cup flour

2 (8-ounce) packages reduced fat cream cheese
1 cup fat-free sour cream
4 egg whites
1 tablespoon vanilla extract

Preheat the oven to 350 degrees. In a bowl, combine the graham cracker crumbs, 1 tablespoon sugar and water, mixing with a fork until well combined. Press into the bottom and up the sides of a deep 10-inch pie plate. In a large mixing bowl,

Continued on next page

beat the sugar, flour and cream cheese until smooth. Add the sour cream, mixing well. Add the egg whites, beating until creamy. Add the vanilla. Pour the filling into the prepared crust. Bake for 40 minutes, or until the filling is just set. Turn off the heat but leave the cake in the oven for 30 minutes longer. Cool on a wire rack and then refrigerate until chilled and ready to serve.

Calories: 240   Cholesterol: 23 mg.   Fat: 7.7 g.   Fat Calories: 29%

Cheesecake Fruit Tart

With cheesecake an all time favorite, you have a guaranteed winner with this dessert. The fresh fruit topping the cheesecake filling makes this tart outstanding and pretty as a picture. Use the fruits of your choice!

1 *(15-ounce) package refrigerated pie crust*	1 *teaspoon almond extract*
1 *(8-ounce) package fat-free cream cheese*	1 *pint fresh blueberries*
3 *tablespoons sugar*	2-3 *nectarines, pitted, peeled and thinly sliced*
½ *teaspoon grated lemon rind*	1 *pint raspberries*
3 *tablespoons almond liqueur, divided*	⅓ *cup apricot preserves*

Preheat the oven to 450 degrees. Arrange the crust in a 9-inch pie tart pan with a removable bottom. Press out the fold lines sealing together any cracks. Fold any excess pastry in forming double thick sides. Bake until brown, about 10 minutes. Cool completely. Meanwhile, in a large mixing bowl, beat together the cream cheese, sugar, lemon rind, 2 tablespoons almond liqueur, and almond extract, blending until smooth. Spread the cheese mixture in the prepared crust. Refrigerate until firm, about 1 hour. Mound the berries in the center of the tart. Arrange the nectarine slices in a ring around the berries. Place the raspberries along the outside edge. In a small saucepan over low heat or in the microwave, stir the apricot preserves until melted. Mix in the remaining 1 tablespoon almond liqueur. Spoon the glaze over the fruit topping. Refrigerate for 2 hours or until well chilled. Yield: 8 to 10 servings.

Calories: 384   Cholesterol: 16 mg.   Fat: 15.1 g.   Fat Calories: 35%

Banana Eclair

When I want an indulgent dessert with a spectacular presentation, this is my first choice. The recipe is a little time consuming but worth the effort. This dessert is showpiece quality with the taste to back it up.

1 cup water	2 large eggs
½ cup margarine	3 large egg whites
1 cup flour	Banana Cream Filling (recipe
2 tablespoons sugar	follows)
	Chocolate Glaze (recipe follows)

Preheat the oven to 400 degrees. In a large saucepan, bring the water and margarine to a boil over a medium heat cooking until the margarine is melted. In a small bowl, combine the flour with the sugar, and add all at once, stirring vigorously with a spoon until the dough forms a ball and leaves the sides of the pan. Remove pan from heat. Beat in the eggs and egg whites with a spoon, one at a time, and continue beating until the dough is stiff and glossy. On a 15 x 10 x 1-inch jelly-roll pan coated with nonstick cooking spray, form about two-thirds of the dough into one long oblong about 7 inches wide. Spoon the reserved dough into mounds along the top of the oblong. Bake for 20 to 25 minutes or until golden brown. Remove from the oven and with a sharp knife, make slits along sides of the eclair about 2 inches apart to let the steam escape. Return to the oven and continue baking for 10 minutes longer. Remove to a cooling rack. Carefully slice off the top of the eclair. It may come off in pieces. Remove and scoop out any soft dough inside the shell. Cool thoroughly. Place the bottom on a serving platter, fill, cover with pieces to form the top if not in whole piece, and drizzle with the glaze. Refrigerate until serving time.

Banana Cream Filling:

2 envelopes whipped topping mix	6-8 bananas
1 cup cold skim milk	¼ cup banana liqueur

In a large mixing bowl, combine both envelopes of the whipped topping and the milk beating until the topping is very thick and forms a peak. Mash enough bananas to make 2 cups and mix with the banana liqueur. Fold the banana mixture into the whipped topping. Fill the bottom eclair shell with half of the whipped topping mixture. Slice the remaining bananas over the topping. Cover with the remaining whipped topping mixture. Replace the top of the eclair or piece together and drizzle with glaze.

Continued on next page

Chocolate Glaze:

1	tablespoon margarine, melted	⅔	cup powdered sugar
2	tablespoons cocoa	3	tablespoons boiling water
1	teaspoon vanilla		

In a small bowl, combine the melted margarine, cocoa, vanilla, and powdered sugar. Stir in the boiling water to make a thin glaze. Drizzle over the filled eclair. Yield: 16 to 20 servings.

Calories: 213   Cholesterol: 27 mg.   Fat: 8.4 g.   Fat Calories: 35%

Chocolate Surprise Dessert

I literally made this dessert in minutes when I had my family coming for dinner. It will satisfy any sweet tooth.

1	(16-ounce) commercially bought angel food cake	¼	cup cocoa
1	(10-ounce) bag large marsh-mallows	1	teaspoon vanilla extract
⅓	cup water	1	cup frozen fat-free whipped topping, thawed

Slice one inch off the top of cake; set aside. Cut out the interior of the cake, removing the interior and leaving wall 1-inch thick on all sides. Dust off the crumbs. Place the cake on a plate. In a medium saucepan, combine marshmallows, water and cocoa. Cook, stirring constantly, over low heat until the marshmallows melt. Add the vanilla. Cool to room temperature. Fold in the whipped topping. Spoon the chocolate mixture into the hollowed portion of the cake; then replace the top section of cake. Refrigerate. If there is any filling left, frost the top of the cake. Yield: 12 to 16 servings.

Calories: 187   Cholesterol: 0 mg.   Fat: 0.4 g.   Fat Calories: 2%

Chocolate Cream Puffs with Mocha Cream Filling

Make the cream puffs the day before and store in zip lock bags. The filling is made with instant pudding to make this elegant dessert one that can be easily made. Garnish with shaved chocolate. The filling is great in a pie too!

1 cup water	1 tablespoon sugar
6 tablespoons margarine	3 large eggs
1 cup flour	2 large egg whites
1 tablespoon cocoa	Mocha Cream Filling (recipe follows)

In a large saucepan, bring the water and margarine to a boil over a medium heat. Combine the flour with the cocoa and sugar; add all at once, stirring vigorously with spoon until the dough forms a ball and leaves sides of pan. Remove from heat. Beat in the eggs and egg whites, one at a time, and continue beating until dough is stiff and glossy. Drop 12 heaping spoonfuls of dough on a baking sheet coated with nonstick cooking spray. Bake at 450 degrees for 15 minutes, reduce heat to 350 degrees and continue baking for another 20 minutes. Remove from oven and with a sharp knife, make a slit horizontally in upper third of each cream puff. Turn off oven and return to oven for 15 minutes so inside of cream puffs with dry out. Cool completely and fill with Mocha Cream Filling. Refrigerate. Yield: 12 cream puffs.

Mocha Cream Filling:

¾ cup skim milk	1 (4-serving) package chocolate
2 tablespoons coffee liqueur	instant pudding and pie filling
1 teaspoon instant coffee	mix
	1 (8-ounce) container frozen fat-free whipped topping, thawed

In bowl, stir together the milk, coffee liqueur, and coffee until coffee is dissolved. Add the pudding mix and beat until it thickens. Gently fold in the whipped topping and fill cream puffs.

Calories: 195   Cholesterol: 54 mg.   Fat: 7.3 g.   Fat Calories: 34%

Strawberry Mousse Parfait with Raspberry Sauce

A refreshing light dessert. The mousse can be poured into a baked pie crust and served with the Raspberry Sauce also. You will find all kinds of uses for this delicious Raspberry Sauce.

2 **envelopes unflavored gelatin**	2 **tablespoons lemon juice**
¼ **cup cool water**	⅓ **cup sugar**
¼ **cup boiling water**	1 **envelope whipped topping mix**
3 **tablespoons Cointreau**	½ **cup cold skim milk**
1 **(16-ounce) package frozen**	½ **teaspoon vanilla**
unsweetened strawberries,	**Raspberry Sauce (recipe follows)**
thawed	

In a small bowl, soften gelatin for 5 minutes in ¼ cup cool water. Add boiling water and stir until gelatin is dissolved. Add Cointreau and mix well. Set aside. In a food processor, purée strawberries. Add lemon juice, sugar and gelatin mixture. Mix well. In mixing bowl, beat together the envelope whipped topping mix, milk, and vanilla; beat until mixture thickens and peaks form (about 4 minutes). Fold whipped topping into strawberry mixture, mixing just until blended. Pour into parfait glasses and refrigerate until firm. Drizzle with Raspberry Sauce (see recipe below) over top of mousse and garnish with fresh strawberries and mint leaves. Yield: 8 to 10 parfaits.

Raspberry Sauce:

1 **(12-ounce) package unsweet-**	¼ **cup sugar**
ened raspberries, thawed	2 **tablespoons lemon juice**
1 **tablespoon Cointreau**	

Purée raspberries in food processor until smooth. Pour through strainer to remove seeds. Add Cointreau, sugar, and lemon juice, mixing well. Refrigerate until serving time.

Calories: 165   Cholesterol: 0 mg.   Fat: 1.3 g.   Fat Calories: 7%

Toffee Torte

These ingredients create a creamy light dessert with a toffee flavoring. Great after a heavy meal.

2   **dozen ladyfingers, halved**
1   **envelope unflavored gelatin**
½   **cup cold water**
1   **(4-serving) package vanilla pudding and pie filling (not instant)**

3   **cups skim milk, divided**
½   **cup chopped English toffee candy bars**
1   **teaspoon vanilla extract**
2   **envelopes whipped topping mix**

In a 9-inch springform pan, stand the ladyfingers upright with the top crust toward the pan. Line the bottom of the pan with more ladyfinger halves; set aside remainder. Soften the gelatin in the cold water; set aside. Prepare the pudding according to package directions using 2 cups milk. Add the gelatin to the prepared hot pudding and stir until dissolved. Stir in the toffee pieces and vanilla. Chill the mixture until it starts to thicken, about 1 hour, stirring occasionally. Prepare the whipped topping with the remaining 1 cup milk according to directions on package. Fold in half of the whipped topping into the chilled toffee mixture. Fill the center of the pan with alternate layers of pudding and the remaining ladyfingers, making the pudding the top layer. Spread with the remaining whipped topping. Refrigerate until firm. To serve, remove the sides of the pan. Yield: 12 servings.

Calories: 204   Cholesterol: 85 mg.   Fat: 5.6 g.   Fat Calories: 26%

Ambrosia Crumble

For this recipe, I suggest using fresh fruit, and for a real treat, serve over frozen vanilla yogurt. This is one of those desserts I attack right when it comes out of the oven.

1 **cup flour**	3 **large navel oranges, peeled and**
½ **cup light brown sugar**	**sectioned**
3 **tablespoons margarine**	3 **large bananas, cut into ½-inch-**
¼ **cup flaked coconut**	**thick slices**
2 **cups fresh pineapple chunks**	2 **tablespoons lemon juice**
	1 **teaspoon coconut extract**

Preheat the oven to 350 degrees. In a bowl, combine the flour and brown sugar; cut in the margarine with a pastry blender or fork until the mixture is crumbly. Set aside. In a bowl, combine the coconut, pineapple, oranges, bananas, lemon juice and coconut extract; toss well. Place the fruit mixture in a 13 × 9 × 2-inch baking dish coated with nonstick cooking spray; sprinkle with the reserved flour mixture. Bake, uncovered, for 45 minutes, until golden. Yield: 10 servings.

Calories: 244   Cholesterol: 0 mg.   Fat: 5.6 g.   Fat Calories: 20%

Blueberry Pineapple Delight

A quick dessert that is perfect for blueberry season. Lemon lovers will have a big smile while enjoying this cobbler type dessert. This is great served hot out of the oven. . . with a little of frozen vanilla yogurt.

1 **(20-ounce) can crushed pine-**	1 **(18.5-ounce) box lemon cake**
apple in juice, undrained	**mix**
2 **cups fresh or frozen blueberries**	⅔ **cup light brown sugar**
	½ **cup margarine, melted**

Preheat the oven to 350 degrees. In a 13 × 9 × 2-inch baking pan coated with nonstick cooking spray, spread the pineapple and blueberries along the bottom of the pan. Sprinkle evenly with the cake mix and brown sugar. Drizzle with the margarine. Bake for 45 to 50 minutes or until bubbly. Yield: 16 servings.

Calories: 254   Cholesterol: 8 mg.   Fat: 9.7 g.   Fat Calories: 33%

Fabulous Fruit Trifle

A truly spectacular presentation that is so easily prepared. Be creative and use your favorite fruit choices and prepare this winner anytime of the year.

2   **(4-serving) packages instant vanilla pudding and pie filling mix**
2½ **cups skim milk**
1   **(8-ounce) package fat-free cream cheese, softened**
1   **(16-ounce) commercially prepared angel food cake, cut into cubes**

¼   **cup almond liqueur, divided**
2   **cups peeled, sliced fresh peaches (about 1 pound)**
2   **large ripe bananas, sliced**
1   **(8-ounce) container frozen fat-free whipped topping, thawed**

In a mixing bowl, combine the pudding mix and milk; beat at low speed of an electric mixer for 2 minutes or until well blended and thickened. Blend in the cream cheese; beat well. Line the bottom of a 2½-quart straight-sided glass bowl or trifle bowl with half of the cake cubes. Drizzle half of the almond liqueur over the cake. Spoon half of the pudding mixture over the cake. Arrange half of the peaches and 1 sliced banana over the pudding mixture. Repeat the layers with the remaining ingredients. Spread with whipped topping to cover and chill at least 3 hours. Yield: 12 servings.

Calories: 272   Cholesterol: 2 mg.   Fat: 0.6 g.   Fat Calories: 2%

Black Forest Trifle

This chocolate lover's dream is very rich and full of dark sweet cherries and chocolate. Trifles serve a crowd, can be prepared ahead of time and are so pretty!

1   *(1 pound 4.5 ounce) box reduced fat fudge brownie mix*
¼   *cup almond liqueur, divided*
1   *(21-ounce) can dark sweet cherry pie filling*
1   *teaspoon almond extract*

2   *(4-serving) boxes instant chocolate pudding and pie filling*
3   *cups skim milk*
1   *(8-ounce) container fat-free frozen whipped topping, thawed*

Preheat the oven to 350 degrees. Prepare the brownie mix according to the package directions. Cool and cut into squares. Place half of the squares in the bottom of a trifle bowl or glass dish. Drizzle the squares with ⅛ cup almond liqueur. Combine the cherry pie filling with the almond extract in the can, stirring well. Spread half the cherry pie filling over the brownies. In a mixing bowl, prepare both packages of the chocolate pudding with the skim milk according to the package directions. Spread half the pudding over the pie filling and top with half of the whipped topping. Repeat the layers ending with the whipped topping. Yield: 16 servings.

Calories: 300   Cholesterol: 1 mg.   Fat: 3.4 g.   Fat Calories: 10%

Banana Pudding Trifle

This is banana pudding taken to the most incredible level. I'm not sure if the presentation or the dessert is the best. Don't let a trifle intimidate you-it is just a layering of ingredients.

1 **cup sugar**	¾ **cup banana liqueur (can use**
¾ **cup all-purpose flour**	**non-alcoholic)**
4 **cups skim milk**	6 **bananas**
2 **large egg yolks, slightly beaten**	2 **(1.4-ounce) English toffee**
1 **tablespoon vanilla extract**	**candy bars, crushed**
1 **(11-ounce) box reduced fat**	1 **(8-ounce) container fat-free**
vanilla wafers	**whipped topping, thawed**

In a large saucepan, combine the sugar and flour. Gradually stir in the milk and bring the mixture to a boil over a medium-high heat, stirring constantly. Place the egg yolks in a small bowl and gradually pour some of the hot custard into the egg yolks mixing well with a fork. Gradually, pour the hot custard mixture back into the saucepan with the remaining custard, cooking over a low heat for several minutes. Do not boil. Remove from the heat and add the vanilla. Transfer the custard to a bowl and allow to cool (can refrigerate to speed up the cooling). In a trifle bowl or a large glass bowl, place one-third of the vanilla wafers; sprinkle with one-third (¼ cup) of the banana liqueur over the wafers. Then, slice 2 of the bananas to place on the wafers. Spread one-half of the custard on top and sprinkle with one-half of the crushed candy bars. Repeat the layers again using all of the remaining custard and crushed candy bars. Then place the final one-third layer of the vanilla wafers, ¼ cup banana liqueur, and 2 sliced bananas and top with the whipped topping. Yield: 16 servings.

Calories: 314   Cholesterol: 30 mg.   Fat: 4.9 g.   Fat Calories: 14%

Strawberry Pie

When strawberries are in season, this pie is one of the best! Of course, if you're in a hurry, you can always cheat and buy a pre-made pie crust.

Crust:

1¼ cups flour
1 tablespoon sugar
½ teaspoon grated lemon peel
Pinch of salt
2 tablespoons canola oil

4 tablespoons ice water
1 (8-ounce) container fat-free frozen whipped topping, thawed
Strawberry Filling (recipe follows)

Preheat oven to 400 degrees. In a large bowl, stir together the flour, sugar, lemon peel and salt. Drizzle with the oil while stirring the mixture with a fork until if forms coarse crumbs. Then stir in the ice water, 1 tablespoon at a time, until mixture begins to pull away from the sides of the bowl. Gather into a ball, roll the dough out and fit it in a 9-inch pie plate. The dough will be slightly crumbly; mend any tears by pressing it together with your fingertips. Cover the pie dough with a clean sheet of wax paper and weight it with dried beans, or raw rice or pie weights. Bake for 10 minutes. Remove the wax paper and weights and continue baking until the crust is golden, about 5 to 10 minutes. Cool on a wire rack. Fill with Strawberry Filling and top with the whipped topping. Yield: 8 servings.

Strawberry Filling:

2 pints ripe strawberries, rinsed and hulled
½ cup sugar

3 tablespoons cornstarch
½ cup water
1 tablespoon lemon juice

Cut 1 pint of the strawberries in half lengthwise for the top of the tart; set aside. Cut the remaining pint into thin slices. In a medium saucepan, combine the sugar and cornstarch, and stir until thoroughly blended. Gradually stir in the water until the mixture is smooth; add half of the sliced strawberries. Cook, stirring constantly and mashing strawberries with back of spoon, until mixture is boiling and thickened, about 10 minutes. Remove from the heat and stir in the remaining sliced strawberries and lemon juice. Cool and spoon the filling into the prepared pie shell. Refrigerate until set. Arrange the reserved strawberry halves, cut side down, on top of the filling in circles.

Calories: 236   Cholesterol: 0 mg.   Fat: 3.9 g.   Fat Calories: 15%

Strawberry Custard Cake

Of course, this cake is best when strawberries are in season. The luscious creamy fillings brings out the best in the fresh berries.

1 (18.5-ounce) box reduced fat yellow cake mix
Glazed strawberries (recipe follows)
Custard Filling (recipe follows)
1 (8-ounce) container frozen fat-free whipped topping, thawed

Preheat oven to 350 degrees. Coat two 9-inch round cake pans with nonstick cooking spray and dust with flour. Follow the directions on the box, and pour the batter evenly into the cake pans. Bake for 30 minutes. Remove from the pans and cool on wire racks. To assemble the cake, put the bottom layer on a serving plate. Top with the Glazed strawberries. Top with the second layer. Frost the sides and top with the whipped topping. Yield: 16 servings.

Glazed Strawberries:

¼ cup water
¼ cup sugar
1 pint strawberries

In a small saucepan, bring the water and sugar to a boil, boiling just until the sugar dissolves. Hull and slice the strawberries in half and place in a bowl. Pour the prepared hot syrup over the strawberries, toss to coat, and refrigerate until chilled. Toss again before filling the cake.

Custard Filling:

3 tablespoons sugar
2 tablespoons cornstarch
⅛ teaspoon salt
1½ cups skim milk
1 egg
1 teaspoon vanilla extract

Combine the sugar, cornstarch, and salt in saucepan. Gradually add milk, stirring until blended. Cook over medium heat, stirring constantly until mixture thickens and comes to a boil. Boil 1 minute, stirring. Remove from heat. Whisk the egg until thick and gradually stir in one fourth hot mixture into beaten egg; return to hot mixture. Cook, stirring constantly, for several minutes. Remove from heat; add vanilla. Cover and chill in refrigerator.

Calories: 217   Cholesterol: 54 mg.   Fat: 3.8 g.   Fat Calories: 16%

German Chocolate Cake

Unbelievably delicious!!! German Chocolate Cake has always been one of my favorites, so I have created this wonderful lighter version for us all to enjoy. This cake does take a little more effort, but it is worth every minute of preparation.

2 **tablespoons cocoa**	½ **teaspoon coconut extract**
2 **ounces German sweet baking**	2 **cups flour**
chocolate	1 **teaspoon baking powder**
½ **cup boiling water**	1 **teaspoon baking soda**
3 **tablespoons margarine**	1 **cup low-fat buttermilk**
2 **tablespoons canola oil**	3 **large egg whites**
2 **cups sugar**	**Coconut Pecan Frosting (recipe**
1 **tablespoon vanilla**	**follows)**

Preheat oven to 350 degrees. Coat three 9-inch round cake pans with nonstick cooking spray and dust with flour. Add cocoa and baking chocolate to the boiling water and stir until melted; set aside to cool slightly. In a mixing bowl, beat together the margarine, oil, and sugar until creamy. Add the vanilla and coconut extracts. Gradually add the chocolate mixture. In another bowl, mix together the flour, baking powder, and baking soda. Add the flour mixture to the creamed mixture alternately with the buttermilk, beginning and ending with the flour mixture. In another mixing bowl, beat the egg whites until stiff peaks form. Gradually fold the egg whites into the chocolate mixture. Pour the batter into the prepared pans. Bake for 20 minutes or until a toothpick inserted comes out clean. Cool in pans 10 minutes and removed to wire racks. Place a layer on a serving plate; spread with one-third the frosting. Top with another layer. Spread with frosting, and top with last layer and spreading remaining frosting over top.

Coconut Pecan Frosting:

1 **(12-ounce) can low-fat evapo-**	2 **teaspoons vanilla extract**
rated milk	½ **teaspoon coconut extract**
⅔ **cup sugar**	½ **cup flaked coconut**
3 **tablespoons cornstarch**	⅓ **cup chopped pecans, toasted**
1 **large egg yolk**	

In saucepan, combine evaporated milk, sugar, cornstarch, and egg yolk. Bring to a boil over medium high heat stirring constantly until mixture thickens and bubbles. Remove from heat and stir in vanilla, coconut extract, coconut and pecans. Cool slightly and frost cake as directed. Yield: 16 servings.

NOTE: To toast pecans, spread evenly in a baking dish and place in oven at 350 degrees for approximately 10 to 15 minutes or until golden brown. Watch carefully as they will burn easily.

Calories: 314   Cholesterol: 18 mg.   Fat: 8.8 g.   Fat Calories: 25%

Sensational Sweet Potato Cake

Move over carrot cake and try this fabulous three layer spicy cake iced with a rich Cream Cheese Frosting. This popular cake is easily prepared with a cake mix.

1 **(18½-ounce) box reduced-fat yellow cake mix**	1 **(15-ounce) can sweet potatoes (yams), drained and mashed (1 cup)**
1 **teaspoon ground cinnamon**	
½ **teaspoon ground nutmeg**	1 **cup drained crushed pineapple**
3 **large eggs**	1 **teaspoon vanilla**
2 **tablespoons canola oil**	**Cream Cheese Frosting (recipe**
1⅓ **cups water**	**follows)**

Preheat the oven to 350 degrees. Coat three 9-inch round cake pans with nonstick cooking spray and dust with flour. In a large mixing bowl, combine the cake mix, cinnamon, nutmeg, eggs, oil, water, sweet potatoes, crushed pineapple and vanilla mixing at a low speed until well combined. Pour into prepared pans. Bake for 20 to 25 minutes or until a toothpick inserted comes out clean. Cool and ice cake with Cream Cheese Frosting. Yield: 16 to 20 servings.

Cream Cheese Frosting:

1 **(8-ounce) package light cream cheese**	1 **(16-ounce) box powdered sugar**
	1 **teaspoon vanilla**
3 **tablespoons margarine**	

In a mixing bowl, blend together the cream cheese and margarine. Gradually add the powdered sugar mixing until smooth. Add vanilla. Blend again.

Calories: 325   Cholesterol: 45 mg.   Fat: 6.9 g.   Fat Calories: 19%

Red Velvet Cake

Yes, this is the recipe we have loved for years, but now you can enjoy it without the guilt. I promise you can't tell the difference from the old fattening version...The perfect holiday cake!

1	(1-ounce) bottle red food coloring	1	cup buttermilk
4	tablespoons cocoa	2¼	cups flour
½	cup margarine	1	teaspoon baking soda
1¾	cups sugar	1½	teaspoons vanilla extract
1	large egg	1	teaspoon butter flavoring
2	large egg whites	1½	teaspoons vinegar
			Special Frosting (recipe follows)

Preheat the oven to 350 degrees. Coat two 9-inch round cake pans with nonstick cooking spray and dust with flour. In a small bowl, mix the red food coloring and cocoa with fork; set aside. In mixing bowl, cream the margarine and sugar until light and fluffy. Add egg and egg whites, mixing well. Add the cocoa mixture to the margarine mixture, beating well. Combine the flour with the baking soda and add alternately with the buttermilk to the creamed mixture, beginning and ending with flour. Add the vanilla, butter flavoring, and vinegar, mixing well. Pour the batter into the pans and bake for 30 minutes or until a toothpick inserted comes out clean. Cool layers on racks and ice with Special Frosting.

Special Frosting:

3	tablespoons flour	½	cup margarine
1	cup skim milk	1	teaspoon vanilla extract
1	cup sugar		

In a small saucepan, gradually stir the milk into the flour and cook over medium heat until very thick, stirring constantly. Cool completely!! In a mixing bowl, beat together the sugar, margarine, and vanilla until light and fluffy. Add the cooled flour mixture; beating well. Spread between layers and on top and sides of cake.

Calories: 328   Cholesterol: 14 mg.   Fat: 12.2 g.   Fat Calories: 33%

Better Than Sex Cake

Here's a familiar recipe that I made lower fat. Keep these ingredients in your pantry to prepare this fabulous cake in a moment's notice. This is a family favorite of mine.

1 **(18½-ounce) box reduced fat yellow cake mix**	1 **(4-serving size) package vanilla instant pudding and pie filling mix**
1 **cup plain nonfat yogurt**	
¾ **cup skim milk**	1 **(4-ounce) bar German sweet chocolate, grated**
2 **tablespoons canola oil**	
2 **large eggs**	⅓ **cup semisweet chocolate chips**
	⅓ **cup pecans, toasted, optional**

Preheat the oven to 350 degrees. Coat a bundt pan with nonstick cooking spray. In a mixing bowl, beat together the cake mix, yogurt, milk, oil, eggs, and vanilla pudding until well mixed. Stir in the grated chocolate, chocolate chips, and pecans. Pour into pan and bake for 50 to 55 minutes or until a toothpick inserted in center comes out clean. Cool 10 minutes; invert on serving plate. Sprinkle with powdered sugar if desired. Yield: 24 servings.

Calories: 153   Cholesterol: 18 mg.   Fat: 4.1 g.   Fat Calories: 23%

Chocolate Swirl Pound Cake

There's nothing better than an old fashioned pound cake and the chocolate swirl makes this cake extra special.

¾ **cup margarine**	1 **teaspoon baking soda**
1¼ **cups sugar**	1 **cup nonfat sour cream**
1 **large egg**	1 **teaspoon vanilla extract**
2 **large egg whites**	¼ **cup light brown sugar**
2 **cups flour**	1 **tablespoon cocoa**
1 **teaspoon baking powder**	½ **teaspoon cinnamon**

Preheat the oven to 350 degrees. In a mixing bowl, cream together the margarine and sugar until light and fluffy. Add the egg and egg whites. In a bowl, mix together the flour, baking powder, and baking soda. Add the dry ingredients alternately with the sour cream, beginning and ending with the flour. Add the vanilla.

Continued on next page

In a small bowl, mix together the brown sugar, cocoa, and cinnamon; set aside. Spread half the batter into a 10-inch bundt pan coated with nonstick cooking spray and dusted with flour. Sprinkle the two-thirds of chocolate mixture onto the batter. Spread the remaining batter over the chocolate and sprinkle with remaining chocolate mixture. Using a knife, swirl the chocolate mixture into the batter. Bake for 35 to 45 minutes or until a toothpick inserted comes out clean. Do not overbake. Cool 10 minutes and then invert onto serving plate. Sprinkle with powdered sugar if desired. Yield: 16 to 20 servings.

Calories: 232   Cholesterol: 15 mg.   Fat: 9.0 g.   Fat Calories: 35%

Chocolate Swirl Angel Food Cake

For those that prefer angel food cake for dessert, the chocolate swirl with the rich chocolate glaze makes this a marvelous cake to remember.

1 **(16-ounce) box angel food cake mix**	**2** **tablespoons cocoa**
	Chocolate Glaze (recipe follows)
2 **tablespoons sugar**	

Preheat the oven to 350 degrees. Prepare the cake according to the directions on the back of the box. In a small bowl, mix together sugar and cocoa; set aside. Spread one-third of the batter into an ungreased 10-inch tube pan. Sprinkle with half of the chocolate mixture. Repeat layering ending with the cake batter. Bake for 35 to 40 minutes or until top is dark golden brown and cracks feel very dry and not sticky. Do not underbake. Cool as directed on package. Invert cooled cake on plate and drizzle with glaze. Yield: 16 servings.

Chocolate Glaze:

2 **tablespoons cocoa**	**1** **tablespoon light corn syrup**
2 **tablespoons water**	**1** **cup powdered sugar**
1 **tablespoon canola oil**	**1** **teaspoon vanilla extract**

In a saucepan, combine the cocoa, water, oil, and corn syrup cooking over a low heat until mixture is smooth; stirring constantly. Remove from heat and add powdered sugar and vanilla, mixing well.

Calories: 156   Cholesterol: 0 mg.   Fat: 1.2 g.   Fat Calories: 6%

Yum Yum Bundt Cake

By pouring the glaze over the cake, it soaks through to make a moist and yummy treat.

1	(18.25-ounce) package box reduced fat yellow cake mix	½	cup almond liqueur, divided
1	(4-serving) box instant pista-chio pudding and pie filling mix	2	large eggs
		2	large egg whites
		¼	cup canola oil
		½	cup nonfat sour cream
1	cup orange juice, divided	½	cup sugar

Preheat the oven to 350 degrees. Coat a 10-inch bundt pan with nonstick cooking spray and dust with flour. In a large bowl, blend together the cake mix, pistachio pudding, ¾ cup orange juice, ¼ cup almond liqueur, eggs, egg whites, oil, and sour cream, beating well. Pour the batter into the pan and bake for 40 minutes to 45 minutes. During the last five minutes of baking, combine the sugar, remaining ¼ cup orange juice and ¼ cup almond liqueur in the microwave proof dish. Micro-wave for 1½ minutes or until mixture boils and sugar is dissolved. Remove cake from oven and pour the mixture over the cake. Let stand for 30 minutes before inverting on servings plate. Yield: 16 to 20 servings.

Calories: 252   Cholesterol: 27 mg.   Fat: 5.0 g.   Fat Calories: 17%

Pineapple Pound Cake

This recipe tastes like an old fashioned pound cake full of butter and eggs. . .with a pineapple twist.

2½	cups flour	1	teaspoon vanilla extract
1½	teaspoons baking soda	1	cup plain nonfat yogurt
½	cup margarine	1	(20-ounce) can crushed pine-apple in own juice, drained
¾	cup sugar		
1	large egg	⅓	cup orange juice
3	large egg whites	¼	cup sugar
1	tablespoon grated orange rind		

Preheat the oven to 350 degrees. In a bowl, combine the flour and baking soda; set aside. In a mixing bowl, beat together the margarine and ¾ cup sugar until light and fluffy. Add the egg, egg whites, orange rind, and vanilla, beating well. Add the

Continued on next page

flour mixture alternately with the yogurt to the sugar mixture, beginning and ending with the flour. Stir in the crushed pineapple. Pour the batter into a 10-inch tube pan coated with nonstick cooking spray. Bake for 40 minutes or until a toothpick inserted comes out clean. Let the cake cool for 5 minutes. Meanwhile, in a small saucepan, combine the orange juice and ¼ cup sugar. Bring to a boil, reduce heat, and simmer for 3 to 5 minutes. Invert cake on serving plate. Pierce it with a fork and spoon orange juice glaze over the top of cake. Yield: 20 servings.

Calories: 162   Cholesterol: 11 mg.   Fat: 5.0 g.   Fat Calories: 28%

Pineapple Upside Down Cake

Sometimes I use crushed pineapple which makes the cake easier to cut and you can even cut into smaller pieces. What a presentation either way!

1 **(20-ounce) can pineapple slices, in unsweetened juice**	1½ **teaspoons baking powder**
	1 **cup sugar**
5 **tablespoons margarine**	1 **large egg**
½ **cup light brown sugar**	3 **large egg whites**
6 **maraschino cherries, halved**	⅛ **teaspoon cream of tartar**
1¼ **cups flour**	1 **teaspoon vanilla extract**

Preheat the oven to 325 degrees. Drain the pineapple, reserving the juice. Melt the margarine in a 9-inch square baking pan in the oven. Spoon out 1 tablespoon margarine; set aside. Add the brown sugar to the pan and spread evenly. Top the sugar with the pineapple slices and cherry halves. In a bowl, combine together the flour, baking powder, and sugar. In a mixing bowl, beat together the egg, ½ cup reserved pineapple juice, reserved 1 tablespoon margarine, and vanilla. Add dry ingredients and mix well. In another bowl, beat the egg whites and cream of tartar until peaks are stiff. Fold the egg whites into the batter and carefully pour over the pineapple in pan. Bake on lowest rack in oven 40 to 45 minutes. Let cake stand for 10 minutes before inverting on serving plate. Yield: 12 servings.

Calories: 234   Cholesterol: 18 mg.   Fat: 5.3 g.   Fat Calories: 20%

Old Fashioned White Cake with Double Chocolate Frosting

My kids like this for a birthday cake, and I made it extra special using two differ-ent chocolate icings. The Chocolate Cream Cheese Icing is super!

2½ **cups flour**	1 **teaspoon butter flavoring**
1½ **tablespoons baking powder**	¼ **teaspoon almond extract**
½ **teaspoon baking soda**	4 **large egg whites**
1⅓ **cups sugar**	**Chocolate Cream Cheese Icing**
4 **tablespoons margarine, softened**	**(recipe follows)**
1 **cup skim milk**	**Chocolate Icing (recipe follows)**
1 **teaspoon vanilla extract**	

Preheat the oven to 350 degrees. In mixing bowl, combine flour, baking powder, baking soda, and sugar. Add the margarine, milk, and flavorings beating until well mixed. In another bowl, beat the egg whites until stiff peaks form. Gently fold the egg whites into the batter. Pour the batter into three 9-inch round cake pans coated with nonstick cooking spray. Bake for 20 minutes or until a toothpick inserted comes out clean. Cool 5 minutes before removing from pan. Cool completely and ice with Chocolate Cream Cheese Icing between the layers and Chocolate Icing on top and sides.

Chocolate Cream Cheese Icing:

3 **ounces fat-free cream cheese**	1½ **cups powdered sugar**
2 **tablespoons margarine**	½ **teaspoon vanilla**
1 **tablespoon cocoa**	

In a mixing bowl, blend the cream cheese and margarine until light. Add cocoa, powdered sugar and vanilla, mixing well. Spread between the layers of cake.

Chocolate Icing:

2 **tablespoons unsweetened cocoa**	¼ **teaspoon butter flavoring**
4 **tablespoons margarine**	1 **(16-ounce) box powdered sugar**
1 **teaspoon vanilla**	4-5 **tablespoons skim milk**

In mixing bowl, combine cocoa, margarine, and flavorings. Gradually add pow-dered sugar and enough milk to make spreading consistency. Frost sides and top of cake.

Calories: 375   Cholesterol: 1 mg.   Fat: 7.6 g.   Fat Calories: 18%

Coconut Cake

Use willpower and wait to cut the cake until refrigerated for several hours as the syrup seeps into the cake and makes this a moist coconut cake yet light with the whipped topping. Garnish with toasted coconut, if desired. The longer it sits in the refrigerator, the better it gets.

1 (18½-ounce) box reduced fat yellow cake mix	**½ cup sugar**
3 large eggs	**1 tablespoon coconut extract**
2 tablespoons canola oil	**⅓ cup flaked coconut**
1⅓ cups water	**1 (8-ounce) container fat-free frozen whipped topping, thawed**
1 (12-ounce) can evaporated skimmed milk	

Preheat the oven to 350 degrees. Coat a 13 × 9 × 2-inch pan with nonstick cooking spray. Prepare the cake mix according to directions on box using the eggs, oil, and water. Bake for 30 minutes or until a toothpick inserted comes out clean. Remove from oven and poke holes in the cake with a toothpick. In a saucepan, combine the milk with sugar, coconut extract, and coconut and bring to a boil. Lower heat and simmer for one to two minutes. Spoon mixture over warm cake allowing it to soak into holes. Cool completely. Top with the whipped topping and refrigerate. Chill overnight. Yield: 18 (3 x 6-inch) servings.

Calories: 200   Cholesterol: 36 mg.   Fat: 3.5 g.   Fat Calories: 16%

Chocolate Sheet Cake

This simple recipe will be a favorite in my house always. I whip it up when I need a pick up dessert to feed a crowd. Sometimes I toast my pecans for extra flavor. Also, note this is made in a cookie sheet style pan so you can make lots of pieces.

2 **cups flour**	1½ **teaspoons vinegar**
1⅔ **cups sugar**	1 **teaspoon baking soda**
½ **cup margarine**	1 **large egg**
¼ **cup cocoa**	2 **large egg whites**
1 **cup water**	1 **teaspoon vanilla extract**
½ **cup skim milk**	**Chocolate Icing (recipe follows)**

Preheat the oven to 400 degrees. Coat a 15 × 10 × 1-inch jelly-roll pan with non-stick cooking spray. In a bowl, combine the flour and sugar. In a saucepan, combine the margarine, cocoa, and water. Cook over a low heat and bring to a boil. Remove from heat and pour over dry ingredients in bowl. Mix together the milk with the vinegar, baking soda, egg, egg whites, and vanilla. Add to the chocolate mixture, mixing well. Pour the batter into the pan and bake for 14 to 18 minutes. Do not overbake. Ice hot cake with Chocolate Icing. Yield: 48 pieces.

Chocolate Icing:

6 **tablespoons margarine**	
¼ **cup cocoa**	1 **teaspoon vanilla extract**
½ **cup skim milk**	⅔ **cup chopped pecans**
1 **(16-ounce) box powdered sugar**	

In a saucepan, combine the margarine, cocoa, and milk and bring to a boil. Add the powdered sugar, vanilla, and pecans; mix well. Spread on hot cake. Let cool and cut into squares.

Calories: 130   Cholesterol: 5 mg.   Fat: 4.7 g.   Fat Calories: 32%

The Ultimate Chocolate Cookie

These chewy rich chocolate cookies are addicting. I store them in my freezer in zip top bags so I have them at all times.

½ **cup margarine, softened**	1 **teaspoon hot water**
½ **cup sugar**	1¼ **cups flour**
½ **cup light brown sugar**	½ **teaspoon baking soda**
1 **large egg**	2 **tablespoons cocoa**
1 **teaspoon vanilla extract**	⅔ **cup semisweet chocolate chips**
1 **teaspoon instant espresso powder**	⅓ **cup chopped pecans, toasted, optional**

Preheat the oven to 350 degrees. In a large mixing bowl, mix by hand the margarine, sugar, and brown sugar. Add the egg and vanilla mixing until creamy. Dissolve the espresso powder in the water and add to the sugar mixture. In a bowl, combine the flour, baking soda, and cocoa and add to the sugar mixture, mixing well. Stir in the chocolate chips and pecans. Drop by teaspoonful onto a baking sheet coated with nonstick cooking spray. Bake for 10 minutes. Yield: 36 cookies.

Calories: 79   Cholesterol: 6 mg.   Fat: 3.7 g.   Fat Calories: 41%

Chocolate Holiday Cookies

The tartness of the cranberries combined with the chocolate makes this cookie a winner. Be creative and add chocolate chips or whatever you like to make this festive cookie your favorite.

½ **cup margarine**	¼ **cup cocoa**
1 **cup sugar**	1 **(7-ounce) jar marshmallow**
1 **large egg**	**creme**
1 **teaspoon vanilla extract**	½ **cup chopped white chocolate**
2 **cups flour**	½ **cup dried cranberries**
½ **teaspoon baking powder**	½ **cup chopped pecans, optional**

Preheat the oven to 350 degrees. In a mixing bowl, cream the margarine and sugar. Add the egg and vanilla, mixing well. In a bowl, combine the flour, baking powder, and cocoa; add to the margarine mixture. Blend in the marshmallow creme, stirring until combined. Stir in the white chocolate, cranberries and pecans. Batter is thick. Drop onto baking sheets coated with nonstick cooking spray. Bake for 10 to 12 minutes. Yield: about 4 dozen cookies.

Calories: 82   Cholesterol: 5 mg.   Fat: 2.7 g.   Fat Calories: 29%

Piña Colada Freeze

This is one of the most versatile and refreshing recipes. Serve in parfait glasses or serve as a milkshake type drink. I leave out the rum extract for my family but you can even add rum. Enjoy this perfect recipe on a warm day.

1 **gallon frozen nonfat vanilla**	1 **cup piña colada mixer (nonal-**
yogurt, softened	**coholic found in liquor section)**
½ **cup sugar**	1½ **teaspoons rum extract, optional**
1 **(20-ounce) can crushed pine-**	
apple in own juice, undrained	

In a food processor or blender, mix together the yogurt and sugar. Add the pineapple, piña colada mixer, and rum extract and blend until smooth. Serve immediately or store in freezer. If mixture is too thick you can add skim milk, pineapple juice, or more piña colada mixer and blend well. Yield: 16 (8-ounce) servings.

Calories: 251   Cholesterol: 0 mg.   Fat: 0.3 g.   Fat Calories: 1%

Index

183

Index

Index

Index

Index

Notes and Extra Recipes

Notes and Extra Recipes

Notes and Extra Recipes

Notes and Extra Recipes

Notes and Extra Recipes

Notes and Extra Recipes

Notes and Extra Recipes

Notes and Extra Recipes

Notes and Extra Recipes

Notes and Extra Recipes

Notes and Extra Recipes

Notes and Extra Recipes

Notes and Extra Recipes

Notes and Extra Recipes

Notes and Extra Recipes

Notes and Extra Recipes

Notes and Extra Recipes

Notes and Extra Recipes